A Choice

by Douglas Dunn

A CHOICE OF
BYRON'S VERSE

selected
with an Introduction by
DOUGLAS DUNN

faber and faber

First published in 1974
by Faber and Faber Limited
3 Queen Square London WCIN 3AU
Reprinted 1979, 1983, 1988 and 1990
Printed in Great Britain by
Richard Clay Ltd, Bungay, Suffolk
All rights reserved

ISBN 0 571 10589 0

821.7
BYR

Contents

[7]

Introduction

The Lord Byron beloved of the English public is the character of Dr. Polidori's anecdote, when, in 1816, they arrived together at Ostend—'As soon as he reached his room, Lord Byron fell like a thunderbolt upon the chambermaid.' Genuine pleasures are to be had by reading of lives so active and passionate in outline. It is still true, however, that one of the great British sports is to observe lives bolder than the average with giggling admiration, moral reserve and contempt.

Popular interest in Byron is, then, predominantly sexual, or scandalous. For those interested in distant historical dissipation, there has been much material to go on. From Greece, during his first visit there, he wrote, 'Tell M. that I have obtained above two hundred,' meaning by that statistic his score of 'coitum plenum et obtabilem.' A matter for some admiration, no doubt; and in recent times, Byron's erotic career has been philosophized by Bernard Grebanier as 'sexual confusion', for his interests were directed at both sexes, with a capacity for devotion, tenderness and ruthlessness as well as an elevated quality of friendship—and these human qualities, virtues in spite of character, find their way into Byron's poems.

The truth about Byron is not crude; it is extreme. To his role of masculine sexual hero, one must also add his influence as 'man of sorrows', which, like his eroticism, is confused, as also is his libertarian fervour—he was an English aristocrat, son of a temperamental highland-woman of noble pretensions and small funds, and was ennobled by luck, and enjoyed the prestige accorded by a title.

Byron's life is so packed with incident—farcical and dramatic—that no attempt can be made to go over it here. There is, in any case, no shortage of biographies.

For all his many positive and assertive actions, his knack of decision—often in a spirit of petulance, and even in the service of evading responsibility—I prefer to see the pattern of Byron's life as tragic. When Professor Wilson Knight calls him 'the last Promethean', the evidence is such that he might almost be believed. I say 'almost', because the comparison of a man with a Titan of Greek mythology brings with it an unacceptable kind of exaggeration; and also because Byron's tragic life appears to have been presented by himself, as if by a dramatist who is his own hero, much of the otherwise Shakespearean play in the style of a French farce. There is something so self-indulgent in Byron (who detested that in others—Keats, for example) that one greets his melancholy with disbelief. 'It is my destiny to ruin all I come near,' he wrote. There may be truth in that; but at the same time, such a confession of extreme personal incompetence is self-pity, and it is spoken by a man who at other times was capable of reform and austerity. Harriet Wilson, the Regency courtesan, offered facetious counsel, indicating that those as worldly as Byron thought they could see through him as a man, even if they were not up to understanding the role of his sorrows in poems. 'Dear Adorable Lord Byron, *don't* make a *coarse* old libertine of yourself . . . When you don't feel quite up to the spirit of benevolence throw away your pen, my love, and take a little *calomel*.' But the same coarse old libertine was to write, 'All my malice evaporates in the effusions of my pen.'

Byron, like Burns, has prodigious *fame*. Like Burns, he

is a poet of his biography, and less a great man of his writing. And, again like the Scots poet, popular interest is such that it devolves on named landmarks, although in Byron's case these are scattered across the geography of an artistocratic *voyageur*. One could follow his path on a route of brass plates, houses, pubs, fish-and-chip shops, trattorie, cinemas (in the Champs-Elysées, for example), tavernas, and hotels. He is also the subject of popular entertainments. On the London stage a few years ago there was a travesty called *The Lord Byron Show*; there have been radio dramas, documentaries, and television profiles; there has recently been a film *Lady Caroline Lamb*, following in the footsteps of *The Prince of Lovers* (1922), and *Bad Lord Byron* (1949). There have also been many novels and plays, the best of them being recent, *A Single Summer with Lord B.* by Derek Marlowe (1969). So Byron's appeal is still as popular as it is strong; his life is of genuine Romantic fascination, good for a histrionic fling, a few cheap laughs. The truth is that Byron's life is so extraordinary that it defeats understanding.

From the purely literary point of view, Byron has fared badly. Few outstanding critics have had much time for him. Eliot and Leavis both contributed influential essays, and while characteristically helpful, neither critic wrote from a sympathetic attachment. Less well known critics, such as W. W. Robson, M. K. Joseph and Andrew Rutherford, have served Byron better, while one of the most striking features of Byron's survival is the work of editors and biographers. Among contemporary poets, W. H. Auden has done more for the right understanding of Byron than any other.

Byron's influence on the development of what is modern in poetry is considerable. I find it difficult to believe that Browning could have written in the way he did without having first been impressed by the spoken plainness of Byron's language in *Don Juan*, although, as is well known, the Romantic poet most loved by Browning was Shelley, whose example he thought himself to have betrayed. Modern poetry in English owes much to Browning. Pound, who saw Browning as a crucial prop in his undertaking to cut away 'the crepuscular spirit in modern poetry', was never a supporter of Byron. In his *ABC of Reading*, he advised students to consider any poem of Byron's for seven obvious flaws in the writing. Pound, however, placed great value (in his criticism) on the French poets of the second half of the nineteenth century. Poets such as Laforgue and Corbière, with their ironic, self-effacing, self-destructive attitudes, can be seen as growing out of the residue of *le byronisme* that infected their predecessors. Vigny, Lamartine, Hugo, Musset, were at various phases Romantic in Byronic ways, and just as aristocratic, while Baudelaire had an early affection for Byron's poems; it is worth pointing out that much of the nineteenth-century French poetry which influenced Eliot and Pound—and Eliot in particular—is a writing of pose, and of poetic gesture, that same stance characteristic of an Age which is found in Byron.

Byron's best intensities are of such a different sort in comparison with what Wordsworth and Keats offer, that they are too frequently ignored. It is quite common to hear it said that one cannot like Wordsworth and Keats *and* Byron; or that it is impossible to admire what is Augustan and satirical in poetry *and* what is Romantic. Byron, owing allegiance to Pope and the standards of the eighteenth century, and also to the age he lived in, seems to have attempted—consciously or unconsciously—to make these alleged incompatibles co-exist in a common-sensical harmony that precluded the vague, but not the mysterious. Except, of course, that this 'harmony', or at least the state of being together in one poem, is often grudged; or said to be the consequence of a split imagination, or a dishonest imagination, or a malicious one. The truth, in my opinion, is that Byron more than any other poet, demonstrates the transition from what had prevailed as the achievement of the immediate past, into what is representative of a present Age. Obdurate preferences and nostalgia can act in creative ways in the minds of innovators and revolutionaries.

A reader of Byron must get used to extremes, and to confusion and what it means in terms of personality and literary history. These extremes are stylistic, erotic, satirical, or the puffery of the sublime; exotic settings on one hand, and London society on the other; comedy, and the frantic melancholy and despair of the Romantic victim.

The last of these, like Byron's Romantic descriptions of mountain scenery, is not something one would want to lose entirely. There has, however, been insufficient space for me to represent Byron by anything from his poetic narratives, although, and this is also true of my opinion of Scott's narrative poems, it is not a kind of writing I am prepared to neglect. *Childe Harold* has also been left alone for the purposes of this selection. However, I have printed an extract from *The Prophecy of Dante*, where Byron defines the poet as 'a new Prometheus for new men'. This appears to be in radical contrast to how he saw himself as the poet of *Don Juan*. Or is it?

In his serious exclamatory vein, or promoting the doomed and defiant Byronic posture in the face of the direly troublous, readers might think of 'the impotence of being earnest'. On the other hand, in his *Don Juan* manner, it is almost obligatory to forget just how much of an originator Byron was. It is an improvisatory poem, comic and serious by turns, a poem that can hold everything, its fortuitous story line like a paradoy of his earlier ways of writing. There is nothing quite like the benign rascality of *Don Juan*, its rapidity and digressive energy. The poem it most reminds me of—and you can laugh at this if you like—is Pound's *Cantos*. If Byron's poems proceed from the luck of his hero, and on no other principle except digression, Pound's poem proceeds from the luck of culture and history, interpreted by as many pertinent digressions. It is perhaps the only way of writing 'a poem of some length' in the modern literary situation.

We know, too, from the splendid Variorum Edition of *Don Juan*, just how much care Byron took with the poem, the many false starts, blottings and excisions he felt it necessary to go through in order to get it right. Admittedly, Byron wrote at speed—one might say that he was temperamentally *fast* as well as loose—but a disturbing commonplace persists. Byron, they say, was no reviser, a gentleman who wrote with ease but a haphazard craftsman, only at his best when at the proper weight, like a professional boxer, or free from catarrhs, piles and hangovers. But Byron is a poet of prodigious skills, used in *Don Juan* for both exotic and demotic purposes; he is the ballroom dancer of the *ottava rima*, a difficult verse form, and one which is still hospitable to contemporary usage—for example, Auden's *Letter to Lord Byron* (a seven line version of the stanza) and James Fenton's *Letter to R. H. S. Crossman*.

Byron has also been thought of as a trivializer of poetic art, as someone who, like Philip Larkin, appears not to take poetry quite seriously enough. Byron's attitude to poetry is not so much rebellious, or original, as sacrilegious. It is probably best summed up by saying that he imitated Horace's *Ars Poetica* at a time when such ideas were implied by recent practice as being against the nature of Romantic poetry.

[16]

He clearly preferred action in life to composition in solitude. 'A man', he wrote, 'ought to do something better for mankind than write verses.' Forgetting for a moment that Byron's influence on important events through both his presence and his writing was real—in the cause of Greek Independence—what his attitude insisted on, and achieved, was a strict, critical, and commonsense standard. His later style, culled from Horace, Dryden, Pope and Johnson, is not a contradiction of earlier 'Byronic' attitudes—although these persist, strangely altered by method and context—but a metamorphosis, and a solution to literary problems he thought important.

Byron is modern in that he was consciously aware of writing in a way worthy of modern life. What he brought to the poetic tradition was a means of expressing the turbulance of personality in a context that still paid honour to the classical elegance of the Augustan era. That context is not only autobiographical, but comic, involving both literary and social satire, a realization of what is important in modern life, and the clear and tender love poetry Byron had been able to write from the very beginning. He described his final style as 'the *that there* sort of writing'——

> Confess, confess, you dog and be candid—that it is the sublime of the *that there* sort of writing—it may be bawdy but is it not good English? It may be profligate but is it not *life*, is it not *the thing*? Could any man have written it who has not lived in the world? and tooled in a post-chaise?—in a hackney coach?—in a gondola?—in a vis-a-vis—on a table?—and under it?

Although such a concentration on *these* particulars does tend to over-play his poem's candid sexuality—the hero is the seduced, not the seducer, or the beneficiary of fantastic good luck, or a tender lover—it is manifestly by the author of *Don Juan*. One is strongly tempted to tone down

[17]

this aspect of Byron, in favour of the kind of praise offered by a character in Disraeli's *Vivian Grey* (1826)—'If one thing was more characteristic of Byron's mind than another, it was his strong, shrewd commonsense—his pure, unalloyed sagacity.'

To that description, I would also add that he was reckless and impulsive, in the decisions of his life and, happily, in the writing of *Don Juan*. Much of the give-away recklessness of *Don Juan* is a literary device, an act, a marvellous act that makes the poem into a floorshow. *Don Juan* is an epic of fiasco; and yet besides comedy of erotic circumstance, there is satirical anger, anti-war indignation, firm assertions in the cause of Greek Independence, political and social digressions. Experience is relied on as the source of writing, drawn on both for exotic details and bitter delineations of contemporary literary life; the poem is bitter, mischievous, sweet and genial. It is full of contradictions.

Byron is, like Hardy and Tennyson, a poet for readers. Voluminous, sometimes profound and moving, more often dazzlingly superficial, fluent, commonsensical and particular, he is in *Don Juan* and *The Vision of Judgment* uninterruptedly readable. For all these reasons he is difficult to abbreviate. So my selection is personal, and cannot be offered as anything approaching an authoritative sifting of what is best in Byron.

The text is based on an 1857 edition, and I have modernized spellings in line with contemporary practice.

She Walks in Beauty

I

She walks in beauty, like the night
   Of cloudless climes and starry skies;
And all that's best of dark and bright
   Meet in her aspect and her eyes:
Thus mellowed to that tender light
   Which heaven to gaudy day denies.

II

One shade the more, one ray the less,
   Had half impaired the nameless grace
Which waves in every raven tress,
   Or softly lightens o'er her face;
Where thoughts serenely sweet express,
   How pure, how dear their dwelling-place.

III

And on that cheek, and o'er that brow,
   So soft, so calm, yet eloquent,
The smiles that win, the tints that glow,
   But tell of days in goodness spent,
A mind at peace with all below,
   A heart whose love is innocent!

It is thought that this poem was inspired by the sight of Lady Wilmot Horton at a ball, dressed in mourning colours, but with numerous spangles on her dress.

Stanzas for Music

There be none of Beauty's daughters
   With a magic like thee;
And like music on the waters
   Is thy sweet voice to me:
When, as if its sound were causing
The charmed ocean's pausing,
The waves lie still and gleaming,
And the lulled winds seem dreaming:

And the midnight moon is weaving
   Her bright chain o'er the deep;
Whose breast is gently heaving,
   As an infant's asleep:
So the spirit bows before thee,
To listen and adore thee;
With a full but soft emotion,
Like the swell of Summer's ocean.

By tradition, this poem, written in March 1816, is addressed to Claire Clairmont.

Stanzas for Music

*'O Lachrymarum fons, tenero sacros
Ducentium ortus ex animo: quater
Felix! in imo qui scatentem
Pectore te, pia Nympha, sensit.'*
                  GRAY's *Poemata*

There's not a joy the world can give like that it takes away,
When the glow of early thought declines in feeling's dull
   decay;

'Tis not on youth's smooth cheek the blush alone, which
    fades so fast,
But the tender bloom of heart is gone, ere youth itself be
    past.

Then the few whose spirits float above the wreck of
    happiness
Are driven o'er the shoals of guilt or ocean of excess:
The magnet of their course is gone, or only points in vain
The shore to which their shivered sail shall never stretch
    again.

Then the mortal coldness of the soul like death itself
    comes down;
It cannot feel for others' woes, it dare not dream its own;
That heavy chill has frozen o'er the fountain of our tears,
And though the eye may sparkle still, 'tis where the ice
    appears.

Though wit may flash from fluent lips, and mirth distract
    the breast,
Through midnight hours that yield no more their former
    hope of rest;
'Tis but as ivy-leaves around the ruined turret wreath,
All green and wildly fresh without, but worn and grey
    beneath.

Oh, could I feel as I have felt,—or be what I have been,
Or weep as I could once have wept, o'er many a vanished
    scene;
As springs in deserts found seem sweet, all brackish
    though they be,
So, midst the withered waste of life, those tears would
    flow to me.

March 1815

Churchill's Grave

A FACT LITERALLY RENDERED

I stood beside the grave of him who blazed
   The comet of a season, and I saw
The humblest of all sepulchres, and gazed
   With not the less of sorrow and of awe
On that neglected turf and quiet stone,
With name no clearer than the names unknown,
Which lay unread around it; and I asked
   The Gardener of that ground, why it might be
That for this plant strangers his memory tasked,
   Through the thick deaths of half a century?
And thus he answered—'Well, I do not know
Why frequent travellers turn to pilgrims so;
He died before my day of Sextonship,
   And I had not the digging of this grave.'
And is this all? I thought,—and do we rip
   The veil of Immortality, and crave
I know not what of honour and of light
Through unborn ages, to endure this blight,
So soon, and so successless? As I said,
The Architect of all on which we tread,
For Earth is but a tombstone, did essay
To extricate remembrance from the clay,
Whose minglings might confuse a Newton's thought
   Were it not that all life must end in one,
Of which we are but dreamers;—as he caught
   As 'twere the twilight of a former Sun,
Thus spoke he,—'I believe the man of whom
You wot, who lies in this selected tomb,
Was a most famous writer in his day,
And therefore travellers step from out their way
To pay him honour,—and myself whate'er

Your honour pleases:'—then most pleased I shook
  From out my pocket's avaricious nook
Some certain coins of silver, which as 'twere
Perforce I gave this man, though I could spare
So much but inconveniently:—Ye smile,
I see ye, ye profane ones! all the while,
Because my homely phrase the truth would tell.
You are the fools, not I—for I did dwell
With a deep thought, and with a softened eye,
On that Old Sexton's natural homily,
In which there was Obscurity and Fame,—
The Glory and the Nothing of a Name.

Diodati 1816

Churchill's Grave: Charles Churchill (1731–64) was a satirist. His
best known poem is 'The Author'. He was buried at Dover, in the
churchyard of St. Martin-le-Grand (now demolished); Byron visited
the site on 25th April 1816, just before he caught the boat for Ostend.
  On the manuscript of this poem, Byron wrote that he intended the
poem as an imitation, and a complimentary one, of Wordsworth;
which is interesting, if one takes into account Byron's later views of
him.

Epistle to Augusta

I

My sister! my sweet sister! if a name
Dearer and purer were, it should be thine.
Mountains and seas divide us, but I claim
No tears, but tenderness to answer mine:
Go where I will, to me thou art the same—
A loved regret which I would not resign.
There yet are two things in my destiny,—
A world to roam through, and a home with thee.

II

The first were nothing—had I still the last,
It were the haven of my happiness;
But other claims and other ties thou hast,
And mine is not the wish to make them less.
A strange doom is thy father's son's, and past
Recalling, as it lies beyond redress;
Reversed for him our grandsire's fate of yore,—
He had no rest at sea, nor I on shore.

III

If my inheritance of storms hath been
In other elements, and on the rocks
Of perils, overlooked or unforeseen,
I have sustained my share of worldly shocks,
The fault was mine; nor do I seek to screen
My errors with defensive paradox;
I have been cunning in mine overthrow,
The careful pilot of my proper woe.

IV

Mine were my faults, and mine be their reward.
My whole life was a contest, since the day
That gave me being, gave me that which marred
The gift,—a fate, or will, that walked astray;
And I at times have found the struggle hard,
And thought of shaking off my bonds of clay:
But now I fain would for a time survive,
If but to see what next can well arrive.

V

Kingdoms and empires in my little day
I have outlived, and yet I am not old;
And when I look on this, the petty spray
Of my own years of trouble, which have rolled

Like a wild bay of breakers, melts away:
Something—I know not what—does still uphold
A spirit of slight patience;—not in vain,
Even for its own sake, do we purchase pain.

VI

Perhaps the workings of defiance stir
Within me—or perhaps a cold despair,
Brought on when ills habitually recur,—
Perhaps a kinder clime, or purer air,
(For even to this may change of soul refer,
And with light armour we may learn to bear,)
Have taught me a strange quiet, which was not
The chief companion of a calmer lot.

VII

I feel almost at times as I have felt
In happy childhood; trees, and flowers, and brooks,
Which do remember me of where I dwelt
Ere my young mind was sacrificed to books,
Come as of yore upon me, and can melt
My heart with recognition of their looks;
And even at moments I could think I see
Some living things to love—but none like thee.

VIII

Here are the Alpine landscapes which create
A fund for contemplation;—to admire
Is a brief feeling of a trivial date;
But something worthier do such scenes inspire:
Here to be lonely is not desolate,
For much I view which I could most desire,
And, above all, a lake I can behold
Lovelier, not dearer, than our own of old.

[25]

IX

Oh that thou wert but with me!—but I grow
The fool of my own wishes, and forget
The solitude which I have vaunted so
Has lost its praise in this but one regret;
There may be others which I less may show;—
I am not of the plaintive mood, and yet
I feel an ebb in my philosophy,
And the tide rising in my altered eye.

X

I did remind thee of our own dear Lake,
By the old Hall which may be mine no more.
Leman's is fair; but think not I forsake
The sweet remembrance of a dearer shore:
Sad havoc Time must with my memory make,
Ere *that* or *thou* can fade these eyes before;
Though, like all things which I have loved, they are
Resigned for ever, or divided far.

XI

The world is all before me; I but ask
Of Nature that with which she will comply—
It is but in her summer's sun to bask,
To mingle with the quiet of her sky,
To see her gentle face without a mask,
And never gaze on it with apathy.
She was my early friend, and now shall be
My sister—till I look again on thee.

XII

I can reduce all feelings but this one;
And that I would not;—for at length I see
Such scenes as those wherein my life begun.
The earliest—even the only paths for me—

Had I but sooner learnt the crowd to shun,
I had been better than I now can be;
The passions which have torn me would have slept;
I had not suffered, and *thou* hadst not wept.

XIII

With false Ambition what had I to do?
Little with Love, and least of all with Fame;
And yet they came unsought, and with me grew,
And made me all which they can make—a name.
Yet this was not the end I did pursue;
Surely I once beheld a nobler aim.
But all is over—I am one the more
To baffled millions which have gone before.

XIV

And for the future, this world's future may
From me demand but little of my care;
I have outlived myself by many a day;
Having survived so many things that were;
My years have been no slumber, but the prey
Of ceaseless vigils; for I had the share
Of life which might have filled a century,
Before its fourth in time had passed me by.

XV

And for the remnant which may be to come
I am content; and for the past I feel
Not thankless,—for within the crowded sum
Of struggles, happiness at times would steal,
And for the present, I would not benumb
My feelings farther.—Nor shall I conceal
That with all this I still can look around,
And worship Nature with a thought profound.

For thee, my own sweet sister, in thy heart
I know myself secure, as thou in mine;
We were and are—I am, even as thou art—
Beings who ne'er each other can resign;
It is the same, together or apart,
From life's commencement to its slow decline
We are entwined—let death come slow or fast,
The tie which bound the first endures the last!

Byron wrote this poem at the Villa Diodati in 1816. Augusta Leigh
gave her permission for its eventual publication in 1830.

The 'grandsire' referred to in the poem is Admiral Byron, who was
famous for having had to handle severe storms on almost every
voyage he made; and hence his nickname, 'Foul-weather Jack'.

Lines on Hearing that Lady Byron was Ill

And thou wert sad—yet I was not with thee;
  And thou wert sick, and yet I was not near;
Methought that joy and health alone could be
  Where I was *not*—and pain and sorrow here!
And is it thus?—it is as I foretold,
  And shall be more so; for the mind recoils
Upon itself, and the wrecked heart lies cold,
  While heaviness collects the shattered spoils.
It is not in the storm nor in the strife
  We feel benumbed, and wish to be no more,
  But in the after-silence on the shore,
When all is lost, except a little life.

I am too well avenged!—but 'twas my right;
  Whate'er my sins might be, *thou* wert not sent

To be the Nemesis who should requite—
  Nor did Heaven choose so near an instrument.
Mercy is for the merciful!—if thou
Hast been of such, 'twill be accorded now.
Thy nights are banished from the realms of sleep.—
  Yes! they may flatter thee, but thou shalt feel
  A hollow agony which will not heal,
For thou art pillowed on a course too deep;
Thou hast sown in my sorrow, and must reap
  The bitter harvest in a woe as real!
I have had many foes, but none like thee;
  For 'gainst the rest myself I could defend,
  And be avenged, or turn them into friend;
But thou in safe implacability
Hadst nought to dread—in thy own weakness shielded,
And in my love, which hath but too much yielded,
  And spared, for thy sake, some I should not spare;
And thus upon the world—trust in thy truth,
And the wild fame of my ungoverned youth—
  On things that were not, and on things that are—
Even upon such a basis hast thou built
A monument, whose cement hath been guilt!
  The moral Clytemnestra of thy lord,
  And hewed down, with an unsuspected sword,
Fame, peace, and hope—and all the better life
  Which, but for this cold treason of thy heart,
Might still have risen from out the grave of strife,
  And found a nobler duty than to part.
But of thy virtues didst thou make a vice,
  Trafficking with them in a purpose cold,
  For present anger, and for future gold—
And buying other's grief at any price.
And thus once entered into crooked ways,
The early truth, which was thy proper praise,
Did not still walk beside thee—but at times,

And with a breast unknowing its own crimes,
Deceit, averments incompatible,
Equivocations, and the thoughts which dwell
    In Janus-spirits—the significant eye
Which learns to lie with silence—the pretext
Of prudence, with advantages annexed—
The acquiescence in all things which tend,
No matter how, to the desired end—
    All found a place in thy philosophy.
The means were worthy, and the end is won—
I would not do by thee as thou hast done!

September 1816

This bitter poem was written in September 1816 (i.e. at roughly the
same time as *Epistle to Augusta*) but not printed until 1832. Its anger
and passion were probably aroused by hearing the separate rumours
regarding the nature of relations between Byron and Augusta, and
Byron and his wife, from Shelley; also, and shortly before the poem
was written, Mme de Stael's attempt to reconcile Lord and Lady
Byron had been confounded by Lady Byron's refusals to have anything
to do with it.

So, We'll Go no More A-roving

I

So, we'll go no more a-roving
    So late into the night,
Though the heart be still as loving,
    And the moon be still as bright.

II

For the sword outwears its sheath,
    And the soul wears out the breast,

[30]

And the heart must pause to breathe,
    And love itself have rest.

III

Though the night was made for loving,
    And the day returns too soon,
Yet we'll go no more a-roving
    By the light of the moon.

Although written in Venice in 1817, this poem was not published until 1830.

Sonnet to George the Fourth

ON THE REPEAL OF
LORD EDWARD FITZGERALD'S FORFEITURE

To be the father of the fatherless,
    To stretch the hand from the throne's height, and raise
    His offspring, who expired in other days
To make thy sire's sway by a kingdom less,—
This is to be a monarch, and repress
    Envy into unutterable praise.
    Dismiss thy guard, and trust thee to such traits,
For who would lift a hand, except to bless?
    Were it not easy, sir, and is't not sweet
    To make thyself beloved? and to be
Omnipotent by mercy's means? for thus
    Thy sovereignty would grow but more complete:
A despot thou, and yet thy people free,
    And by the heart, not hand, enslaving us.

Bologna, August 12th, 1819

On This Day I Complete My Thirty-sixth Year

MISSOLONGHI, JAN. 22ND, 1824

'Tis time this heart should be unmoved,
   Since others it hath ceased to move:
Yet, though I cannot be beloved,
      Still let me love!

My days are in the yellow leaf;
   The flowers and fruits of love are gone;
The worm, the canker, and the grief
      Are mine alone!

The fire that on my bosom preys
   Is lone as some volcanic isle;
No torch is kindled at its blaze—
      A funeral pile.

The hope, the fear, the jealous care,
   The exalted portion of the pain
And power of love, I cannot share,
      But wear the chain.

But 'tis not *thus*—and 'tis not *here*—
   Such thoughts should shake my soul, nor *now*
Where glory decks the hero's bier,
      Or binds his brow.

The sword, the banner, and the field,
   Glory and Greece, around me see!
The Spartan, borne upon his shield,
      Was not more free.

Awake! (not Greece—she *is* awake!)
   Awake, my spirit! Think through *whom*
Thy life-blood tracks its parent lake,
      And then strike home!

Tread those reviving passions down,
   Unworthy manhood!—unto thee
Indifferent should the smile or frown
      Of beauty be.

If thou regret'st thy youth, *why live?*
   The land of honourable death
Is here:—up to the field, and give
      Away thy breath!

Seek out—less often sought than found—
   A soldier's grave, for thee the best;
Then look around, and choose thy ground,
      And take thy rest.

from

The Prophecy of Dante

Canto IV, lines 1–19

THE POET

Many are poets who have never penned
   Their inspiration, and perchance the best:
   They felt, and loved, and died, but would not lend
Their thoughts to meaner beings; they compressed
   The god within them, and rejoined the stars

Unlaurelled upon earth, but far more blessed
Than those who are degraded by the jars
    Of passion, and their frailties linked to fame,
    Conquerors of high renown, but full of scars.
Many are poets but without the name,
    For what is poesy but to create
    From overfeeling good or ill; and aim
At an external life beyond our fate,
    And be the new Prometheus of new men,
    Bestowing fire from heaven, and then, too late,
Finding the pleasure given repaid with pain,
    And vultures to the heart of the bestower,
    Who, having lavished his high gift in vain,
Lies chained to his lone rock by the sea-shore?

1819

from

The Curse of Minerva

lines 123–56

A LOUSY SCOTCH PEER
PINCHES THE MARBLES

She ceased awhile, and thus I dared reply,
To soothe the vengeance kindling in her eye:
'Daughter of Jove! in Britain's injured name,
A true-born Briton may the deed disclaim.
Frown not on England; England owns him not:
Athena, no! thy plunderer was a Scot.
Ask'st thou the difference? From fair Phyles' towers
Survey Bœotia;—Caledonia's ours.

[34]

And well I know within that bastard land
Hath Wisdom's goddess never held command;
A barren soil, where Nature's germs, confined
To stern sterility, can stint the mind;
Whose thistle well betrays the niggard earth,
Emblem of all to whom the land gives birth;
Each genial influence nurtured to resist;
A land of meanness, sophistry, and mist.
Each breeze from foggy mount and marshy plain
Dilutes with drivel every drizzly brain,
Till, burst at length, each watery head o'erflows,
Foul as their soil, and frigid as their snows.
Then thousand schemes of petulance and pride
Despatch her scheming children far and wide:
Some east, some west, some every where but north,
In quest of lawless gain, they issue forth.
And thus—accursed be the day and year!
She sent a Pict to play the felon here.
Yet Caledonia claims some native worth,
As dull Bœotia gave a Pindar birth;
So may her few, the lettered and the brave,
Bound to no clime, and victors of the grave,
Shake off the sordid dust of such a land,
And shine like children of a happier strand;
As once, of yore, in some obnoxious place,
Ten names (if found) have saved a wretched race.'

Athens, Capuchin Convent, 17th March, 1811

Byron is writing here about Lord Elgin. Byron's remarks on the
nature of Scotland are interesting in view of the adoption of Byron as
a Scottish poet by 'Hugh MacDiarmid' and his followers.

Windsor Poetics

Lines composed on the occasion of His Royal Highness the Prince Regent being seen standing between the coffins of Henry VIII and Charles I, in the royal vault at Windsor.

Famed for contemptuous breach of sacred ties,
By headless Charles see heartless Henry lies;
Between them stands another sceptred thing—
It moves, it reigns—in all but name, a king:

Charles to his people, Henry to his wife,
—In him the double tyrant start to life:
Justice and death have mixed their dust in vain,
Each royal vampire wakes to life again.
Ah, what can tombs avail!—since these disgorge
The blood and dust of both—to mould a George.

Stanzas

When a man hath no freedom to fight for at home,
   Let him combat for that of his neighbours;
Let him think of the glories of Greece and of Rome,
   And get knocked on the head for his labours.

To do good to mankind is the chivalrous plan,
   And is always as nobly requited;
Then battle for freedom wherever you can,
   And, if not shot or hanged, you'll get knighted.

November, 1820

JOHN KEATS

Who killed John Keats?
  'I,' says the Quarterly,
So savage and Tartarly;
  ' 'Twas one of my feats.'

Who shot the arrow?
  'The poet priest Milman
(So ready to kill man),
  'Or Southey, or Barrow.'

July, 1821

EPIGRAM

FROM THE FRENCH OF RULHIERES

If for silver, or for gold,
  You could melt ten thousand pimples
  Into half a dozen dimples,
Then your face we might behold,
  Looking, doubtless, much more snugly;
Yet even *then* 'twould be d——d ugly.

12th August, 1819

ON MY WEDDING DAY

Here's a happy new year! but with reason
  I beg you'll permit me to say—
Wish me *many* returns of the *season*,
  But as *few* as you please of the *day*.

2nd January, 1820

[37]

EPIGRAM

The world is a bundle of hay,
  Mankind are the asses who pull;
Each tugs it a different way,
  And the greatest of all is John Bull.

EPIGRAM

Oh, Castlereagh! thou art a patriot now;
Cato died for his country, so didst thou:
He perished rather than see Rome enslaved,
Thou cutt'st thy throat that Britain may be saved!

EPITAPH

Posterity will ne'er survey
  A nobler grave than this:
Here lie the bones of Castlereagh:
  Stop, traveller——

[*and piss*] *I mention this, just in case . . .*

from

Hints from Horace

lines 541–69

[A 'translation' of Horace's *Epistolam ad Pisones*, known as
Ars Poetica]

ADVICE TO YOUNG AUTHORS

Young men with aught but elegance dispense;
Maturer years require a little sense.
To end at once:—that bard for all is fit
Who mingles well instruction with his wit;
For him reviews shall smile, for him o'erflow
The patronage of Paternoster-row;
His book, with Longman's liberal aid, shall pass;
(Who ne'er despises books that bring him brass)
Through three long weeks of taste the London lead,
And cross St. George's Channel and the Tweed.

But every thing has faults, nor is't unknown
That harps and fiddles often lose their tone,
And wayward voices, at their owner's call,
With all his best endeavours, only squall;
Dogs blink their covey, flints withhold the spark,
And double-barrels (damn them!) miss their mark.

Where frequent beauties strike the reader's view,
We must not quarrel for a blot or two;
But pardon equally to books or men,
The slips of human nature, and the pen.

Yet if an author, spite of foe or friend,
Despises all advice too much to mend,

But ever twangs the same discordant string,
Give him no quarter, howsoe'er he sing.
Let Havard's fate o'ertake him, who, for once,
Produced a play too dashing for a dunce:
At first none deemed it his; but when his name
Announced the fact—what then?—it lost its fame.
Though all deplore when Milton deigns to doze,
In a long work 'tis fair to steal repose.

Beppo

I

'Tis known, at least it should be, that throughout
   All countries of the Catholic persuasion,
Some weeks before Shrove Tuesday comes about,
   The people take their fill of recreation,
And buy repentance, ere they grow devout,
   However high their rank, or low their station,
With fiddling, feasting, dancing, drinking, masquing,
And other things which may be had for asking.

II

The moment night with dusky mantle covers
   The skies (and the more duskily the better),
The times less liked by husbands than by lovers
   Begins, and prudery flings aside her fetter;
And gaiety on restless tiptoe hovers,
   Giggling with all the gallants who beset her;
And there are songs and quavers, roaring, humming,
Guitars, and every other sort of strumming.

And there are dresses splendid, but fantastical,
   Masks of all times and nations, Turks and Jews,
And harlequins and clowns, with feats gymnastical,
   Greeks, Romans, Yankee-doodles, and Hindoos;
All kinds of dress, except the ecclesiastical,
   All people, as their fancies hit, may choose,
But no one in these parts may quiz the clergy,—
Therefore take heed, ye Freethinkers! I charge ye.

IV

You'd better walk about begirt with briars,
   Instead of coat and smallclothes, than put on
A single stitch reflecting upon friars,
   Although you swore it only was in fun;
They'd haul you o'er the coals, and stir the fires
   Of Phlegethon with every mother's son,
Nor say one mass to cool the caldron's bubble
That boiled your bones, unless you paid them double.

V

But saving this, you may put on whate'er
   You like by way of doublet, cape or cloak,
Such as in Monmouth-street, or in Rag Fair,
   Would rig you out in seriousness or joke;
And even in Italy such places are,
   With prettier name in softer accents spoke,
For, bating Covent Garden, I can hit on
No place that's called 'Piazza' in Great Britain.

VI

This feast is named the Carnival, which being
   Interpreted, implies 'farewell to flesh:'
So called, because the name and thing agreeing,
   Through Lent they live on fish both salt and fresh.

But why they usher Lent with so much glee in,
  Is more than I can tell, although I guess
'Tis as we take a glass with friends at parting,
In the stage-coach or packet just at starting.

VII

And thus they bid farewell to carnal dishes,
  And solid meats, and highly spiced ragouts,
To live for forty days on ill-dressed fishes,
  Because they have no sauces to their stews;
A thing which causes many 'poohs' and 'pishes,'
  And several oaths (which would not suit the Muse),
From travellers accustomed from a boy
To eat their salmon, at the least, with soy;

VIII

And therefore humbly I would recommend
  'The curious in fish-sauce,' before they cross
The sea, to bid their cook, or wife, or friend,
  Walk or ride to the Strand, and buy in gross
(Or if set out beforehand, these may send
  By any means least liable to loss),
Ketchup, Soy, Chili-vinegar, and Harvey,
Or, by the Lord! a Lent will well nigh starve ye;

IX

That is to say, if your religion's Roman,
  And you at Rome would do as Romans do,
According to the proverb,—although no man,
  If foreign, is obliged to fast; and you,
If Protestant, or sickly, or a woman,
  Would rather dine in sin on a ragout—
Dine and be d——d! I don't mean to be coarse,
But that's the penalty, to say no worse.

[42]

X

Of all the places where the Carnival
  Was most facetious in the days of yore,
For dance, and song, and serenade, and ball,
  And masque, and mime, and mystery, and more
Than I have time to tell now, or at all,
  Venice the bell from every city bore,—
And at the moment when I fix my story,
That sea-born city was in all her glory.

XI

They've pretty faces yet, those same Venetians,
  Black eyes, arched brows, and sweet expressions still;
Such as of old were copied from the Grecians,
  In ancient arts by moderns mimicked ill;
And like so many Venuses of Titian's
  (The best's at Florence—see it, if ye will,)
They look when leaning over the balcony,
Or stepped from out a picture by Giorgione,

XII

Whose tints are truth and beauty at their best;
  And when you to Manfrini's palace go,
That picture (howsoever fine the rest)
  Is loveliest to my mind of all the show;
It may perhaps be also to *your* zest,
  And that's the cause I rhyme upon it so:
'Tis but a portrait of his son, and wife,
And self; but *such* a woman! love in life!

XIII

Love in full life and length, not love ideal,
  No, nor ideal beauty, that fine name,
But something better still, so very real,
  That the sweet model must have been the same;

[43]

A thing that you would purchase, beg, or steal,
  Wer't not impossible, besides a shame:
The face recalls some face, as 'twere with pain,
You once have seen, but ne'er will see again;

XIV

One of those forms which flit by us, when we
  Are young, and fix our eyes on every face;
And, oh! the loveliness at times we see
  In momentary gliding, the soft grace,
The youth, the bloom, the beauty which agree,
  In many a nameless being we retrace,
Whose course and home we knew not, nor shall know,
Like the lost Pleiad seen no more below.

XV

I said that like a picture by Giorgione
  Venetian women were, and so they *are*,
Particularly seen from a balcony,
  (For beauty's sometimes best set off afar)
And there, just like a heroine of Goldoni,
  They peep from out the blind, or o'er the bar;
And truth to say, they're mostly very pretty,
And rather like to show it, more's the pity!

XVI

For glances beget ogles, ogles sighs,
  Sighs wishes, wishes words, and words a letter,
Which flies on wings of light-heeled Mercuries,
  Who do such things because they know no better;
And then, God knows what mischief may arise,
  When love links two young people in one fetter,
Vile assignations, and adulterous beds,
Elopements, broken vows, and hearts, and heads.

XVII

Shakespeare described the sex in Desdemona
  As very fair, but yet suspect in fame,
And to this day from Venice to Verona
  Such matters may be probably the same,
Except that since those times was never known a
  Husband whom mere suspicion could inflame
To suffocate a wife no more than twenty,
Because she had a 'cavalier servente.'

XVIII

Their jealousy (if they are ever jealous)
  Is of a fair complexion altogether,
Not like that sooty devil of Othello's,
  Which smothers women in a bed of feather,
But worthier of these much more jolly fellows,
  When weary of the matrimonial tether
His head for such a wife no mortal bothers,
But takes at once another, or another's.

XIX

Didst ever see a Gondola? For fear
  You should not, I'll describe it you exactly:
'Tis a long covered boat that's common here,
  Carved at the prow, built lightly, but compactly,
Rowed by two rowers, each called 'Gondolier,'
  It glides along the water looking blackly,
Just like a coffin clapt in a canoe,
Where none can make out what you say or do.

XX

And up and down the long canals they go,
  And under the Rialto shoot along,
By night and day, all paces, swift or slow,
  And round the theatres, a sable throng,

They wait in their dusk livery of woe,—
   But not to them do woeful things belong,
For sometimes they contain a deal of fun,
Like mourning coaches when the funeral's done.

XXI

But to my story.—'Twas some years ago,
   It may be thirty, forty, more or less,
The Carnival was at its height, and so
   Were all kinds of buffoonery and dress;
A certain lady went to see the show,
   Her real name I know not, nor can guess,
And so we'll call her Laura, if you please,
Because it slips into my verse with ease.

XXII

She was not old, nor young, nor at the years
   Which certain people call a *'certain age,'*
Which yet the most uncertain age appears,
   Because I never heard, nor could engage
A person yet by prayers, or bribes, or tears,
   To name, define by speech, or write on page,
The period meant precisely by that word,—
Which surely is exceedingly absurd.

XXIII

Laura was blooming still, had made the best
   Of time, and time returned the compliment,
And treated her genteelly, so that, dressed,
   She looked extremely well where'er she went;
A pretty woman is a welcome guest,
   And Laura's brow a frown had rarely bent;
Indeed, she shone all smiles, and seemed to flatter
Mankind with her black eyes for looking at her.

[46]

XXIV

She was a married women; 'tis convenient,
  Because in Christian countries 'tis a rule
To view their little slips with eyes more lenient;
  Whereas if single ladies play the fool,
(Unless within the period intervenient
  A well-timed wedding makes the scandal cool)
I don't know how they ever can get over it,
Except they manage never to discover it.

XXV

Her husband sailed upon the Adriatic,
  And made some voyages, too, in other seas,
And when he lay in quarantine for pratique
  (A forty days' precaution 'gainst disease),
His wife would mount, at times, her highest attic,
  For thence she could discern the ship with ease:
He was a merchant trading to Aleppo,
His name Giuseppe, called more briefly, Beppo.

XXVI

He was a man as dusky as a Spaniard,
  Sunburnt with travel, yet a portly figure;
Though coloured, as it were, within a tanyard,
  He was a person both of sense and vigour—
A better seaman never yet did man yard;
  And she, although her manners showed no rigour,
Was deemed a woman of the strictest principle,
So much as to be thought almost invincible.

XXVII

But several years elapsed since they had met;
  Some people thought the ship was lost, and some
That he had somehow blundered into debt,
  And did not like the thought of steering home;

And there were several offered any bet,
    Or that he would, or that he would not come;
For most men (till by losing rendered sager)
Will back their own opinions with a wager.

XXVIII

'Tis said that their last parting was pathetic,
    As partings often are, or ought to be,
And their presentiment was quite prophetic,
    That they should never more each other see,
(A sort of morbid feeling, half poetic,
    Which I have known occur in two or three,)
When kneeling on the shore upon her sad knee
He left this Adriatic Ariadne.

XXIX

And Laura waited long, and wept a little,
    And thought of wearing weeds, as well she might;
She almost lost all appetite for victual,
    And could not sleep with ease alone at night;
She deemed the window-frames and shutters brittle
    Against a daring housebreaker or sprite,
And so she thought it prudent to connect her
With a vice-husband, *chiefly to protect her*.

XXX

She chose, (and what is there they will not choose,
    If only you will but oppose their choice?)
Till Beppo should return from his long cruise,
    And bid once more her faithful heart rejoice,
A man some women like, and yet abuse—
    A coxcomb was he by the public voice;
A Count of wealth, they said, as well as quality,
And in his pleasures of great liberality.

[48]

And then he was a Count, and then he knew
  Music, and dancing, fiddling, French and Tuscan;
The last not easy, be it known to you,
  For few Italians speak the right Etruscan.
He was a critic upon operas, too,
  And knew all niceties of sock and buskin;
And no Venetian audience could endure a
Song, scene, or air, when he cried 'seccatura!'

His 'bravo' was decisive, for that sound
  Hushed 'Academie' sighed in silent awe;
The fiddlers trembled as he looked around,
  For fear of some false note's detected flaw;
The 'prima donna's' tuneful heart would bound,
  Dreading the deep damnation of his 'bah!'
Soprano, basso, even the contra-alto,
Wished him five fathom under the Rialto.

He patronised the Improvisatori,
  Nay, could himself extemporise some stanzas,
Wrote rhymes, sang songs, could also tell a story,
  Sold pictures, and was skilful in the dance as
Italians can be, though in this their glory
  Must surely yield the palm to that which France has;
In short, he was a perfect cavaliero,
And to his very valet seemed a hero.

Then he was faithful too, as well as amorous;
  So that no sort of female could complain,
Although they're now and then a little clamorous,

[49]

He never put the pretty souls in pain;
His heart was one of those which most enamour us,
   Wax to receive, and marble to retain:
He was a lover of the good old school,
Who still become more constant as they cool.

XXXV

No wonder such accomplishments should turn
   A female head, however sage and steady—
With scarce a hope that Beppo could return,
   In law he was almost as good as dead, he
Nor sent, nor wrote, nor showed the least concern,
   And she had waited several years already;
And really if a man won't let us know
That he's alive, he's *dead*, or should be so.

XXXVI

Besides, within the Alps, to every woman,
   (Although, God knows, it is a grievous sin,)
'Tis, I may say, permitted to have *two* men;
   I can't tell who first brought the custom in,
But 'Cavalier Serventes' are quite common,
   And no one notices nor cares a pin;
And we may call this (not to say the worst)
A *second* marriage which corrupts the *first*.

XXXVII

The word was formerly a 'Cicisbeo,'
   But *that* is now grown vulgar and indecent;
The Spaniards call the person a '*Cortejo*,'
   For the same mode subsists in Spain, though recent;
In short it reaches from the Po to Teio,
   And may perhaps at last be o'er the sea sent:
But Heaven preserve Old England from such courses!
Or what becomes of damage and divorces?

[50]

However, I still think, with all due deference
  To the fair *single* part of the creation,
That married ladies should preserve the preference
  In *tête à tête* or general conversation—
And this I say without peculiar reference
  To England, France, or any other nation—
Because they know the world, and are at ease,
And being natural, naturally please.

XXXIX

'Tis true, your budding Miss is very charming,
  But shy and awkward at first coming out,
So much alarmed, that she is quite alarming,
  All Giggle, Blush; half Pertness, and half Pout;
And glancing at *Mamma*, for fear there's harm in
  What you, she, it, or they, may be about,
The Nursery still lisps out in all they utter—
Besides, they always smell of bread and butter.

XL

But 'Cavalier Servente' is the phrase
  Used in politest circles to express
This supernumerary slave, who stays
  Close to the lady as a part of dress,
Her word the only law which he obeys.
  His is no sinecure, as you may guess;
Coach, servants, gondola, he goes to call,
And carries fan and tippet, gloves and shawl.

XLI

With all its sinful doings, I must say,
  That Italy's a pleasant place to me,
Who love to see the Sun shine every day,
  And vines (not nailed to walls) from tree to tree

[51]

Festooned, much like the back scene of a play,
    Or melodrame, which people flock to see,
When the first act is ended by a dance
In vineyards copied from the south of France.

XLII

I like on Autumn evenings to ride out,
    Without being forced to bid my groom be sure
My cloak is round his middle strapped about,
    Because the skies are not the most secure;
I know too that, if stopped upon my route,
    Where the green alleys windingly allure,
Reeling with grapes red wagons choke the way,—
In England 'twould be dung, dust, or a dray.

XLIII

I also like to dine on becaficas,
    To see the Sun set, sure he'll rise to-morrow,
Not through a misty morning twinkling weak as
    A drunken man's dead eye in maudlin sorrow,
But with all Heaven t'himself; the day will break as
    Beauteous as cloudless, nor be forced to borrow
That sort of farthing candlelight which glimmers
Where reeking London's smoky cauldron simmers.

XLIV

I love the language, that soft bastard Latin,
    Which melts like kisses from a female mouth,
And sounds as if it should be writ on satin,
    With syllables which breathe of the sweet South,
And gentle liquids gliding all so pat in,
    That not a single accent seems uncouth,
Like our harsh northern whistling, grunting guttural,
Which we're obliged to hiss, and spit, and splutter all.

[52]

XLV

I like the women too (forgive my folly),
  From the rich peasant cheek of ruddy bronze,
And large black eyes that flash on you a volley
  Of rays that say a thousand things at once,
To the high dama's brow, more melancholy,
  But clear, and with a wild and liquid glance,
Heart on her lips, and soul within her eyes,
Soft as her clime, and sunny as her skies.

XLVI

Eve of the land which still is Paradise!
  Italian beauty didst thou not inspire
Raphael, who died in thy embrace, and vies
  With all we know of Heaven, or can desire,
In what he hath bequeathed us?—in what guise,
  Though flashing from the fervour of the lyre,
Would *words* describe thy past and present glow,
While yet Canova can create below?

XLVII

'England! with all thy faults I love thee still,'
  I said at Calais, and have not forgot it;
I like to speak and lucubrate my fill;
  I like the government (but that is not it);
I like the freedom of the press and quill;
  I like the Habeas Corpus (when we've got it)
I like a parliamentary debate,
Particularly when 'tis not too late;

XLVIII

I like the taxes, when they're not too many
  I like a seacoal fire, when not too dear;
I like a beef-steak, too, as well as any;
  Have no objection to a pot of beer;

[53]

I like the weather when it is not rainy,
  That is, I like two months of every year.
And so God save the Regent, Church, and King!
Which means that I like all and every thing.

XLIX

Our standing army, and disbanded seamen,
  Poor's rate, Reform, my own, the nation's debt,
Our little riots just to show we're free men,
  Our trifling bankruptcies in the Gazette,
Our cloudy climate, and our chilly women,
  All these I can forgive, and those forget,
And greatly venerate our recent glories,
And wish they were not owing to the Tories.

L

But to my tale of Laura,—for I find
  Digression is a sin, that by degrees
Becomes exceeding tedious to my mind,
  And, therefore, may the reader too displease—
The gentle reader, who may wax unkind,
  And caring little for the author's ease,
Insist on knowing what he means, a hard
And hapless situation for a bard.

LI

Oh that I had the art of easy writing
  What should be easy reading! could I scale
Parnassus, where the Muses sit inditing
  Those pretty poems never known to fail,
How quickly would I print (the world delighting)
  A Grecian, Syrian, or Assyrian tale;
And sell you, mixed with western sentimentalism,
Some samples of the finest Orientalism.

LII

But I am but a nameless sort of person,
  (A broken Dandy lately on my travels)
And take for rhyme, to hook my rambling verse on,
  The first that Walker's Lexicon unravels,
And when I can't find that, I put a worse on,
  Not caring as I ought for critics' cavils;
I've half a mind to tumble down to prose,
But verse is more in fashion—so here goes.

LIII

The Count and Laura made their new arrangement,
  Which lasted, as arrangements sometimes do,
For half a dozen years without estrangement;
  They had their little differences, too;
Those jealous whiffs, which never any change meant;
  In such affairs there probably are few
Who have not had this pouting sort of squabble,
From sinners of high station to the rabble.

LIV

But, on the whole, they were a happy pair,
  As happy as unlawful love could make them;
The gentleman was fond, the lady fair,
  Their chains so slight, 'twas not worth while to break
        them:
The world beheld them with indulgent air;
  The pious only wished 'the devil take them!'
He took them not; he very often waits,
And leaves old sinners to be young ones' baits.

LV

But they were young: Oh! what without our youth
  Would love be! What would youth be without love!
Youth lends its joy, and sweetness, vigour, truth,

[55]

Heart, soul, and all that seems as from above;
But, languishing with years, it grows uncouth—
    One of few things experience don't improve,
Which is, perhaps, the reason why old fellows
Are always so preposterously jealous.

LVI

It was the Carnival, as I have said
    Some six and thirty stanzas back, and so
Laura the usual preparations made,
    Which you do when your mind's made up to go
To-night to Mrs. Boehm's masquerade,
    Spectator, or partaker in the show;
The only difference known between the cases
Is—*here*, we have six weeks of 'varnished faces.'

LVII

Laura, when dressed, was (as I sang before)
    A pretty woman as was ever seen,
Fresh as the Angel o'er a new inn door,
    Or frontispiece of a new Magazine,
With all the fashions which the last month wore,
    Coloured, and silver paper leaved between
That and the title-page, for fear the press
Should soil with parts of speech the parts of dress.

LVIII

They went to the Ridotto;—'tis a hall
    Where people dance, and sup, and dance again;
Its proper name, perhaps, were a masqued ball,
    But that's of no importance to my strain;
'Tis (on a smaller scale) like our Vauxhall,
    Excepting that it can't be spoilt by rain;
The company is 'mixed' (the phrase I quote is
As much as saying, they're below your notice);

[56]

LIX

For a 'mixed company' implies that, save
   Yourself and friends, and half a hundred more,
Whom you may bow to without looking grave,
   The rest are but a vulgar set, the bore
Of public places, where they basely brave
   The fashionable stare of twenty score
Of well-bred persons, called '*The World;*' but I,
Although I know them, really don't know why.

LX

This is the case in England; at least was
   During the dynasty of Dandies, now
Perchance succeeded by some other class
   Of imitated imitators:—how
Irreparably soon decline, alas!
   The demagogues of fashion: all below
Is frail; how easily the world is lost
By love, or war, and now and then by frost!

LXI

Crushed was Napoleon by the northern Thor,
   Who knocked his army down with icy hammer,
Stopped by the *elements*, like a whaler, or
   A blundering novice in his new French grammar;
Good cause had he to doubt the chance of war,
   And as for Fortune—but I dare not d—n her,
Because, were I to ponder to infinity,
The more I should believe in her divinity.

LXII

She rules the present, past, and all to be yet,
   She gives us luck in lotteries, love and marriage;
I cannot say that she's done much for me yet;
   Not that I mean her bounties to disparage,

[57]

We've not yet closed accounts, and we shall see yet
  How much she'll make amends for past miscarriage;
Meantime the Goddess I'll no more importune,
Unless to thank her when she's made my fortune.

LXIII
To turn,—and to return;—the devil take it!
  This story slips for ever through my fingers,
Because, just as the stanza likes to make it,
  It needs must be—and so it rather lingers;
This form of verse began, I can't well break it,
  But must keep time and tune like public singers;
But if I once get through my present measure,
I'll take another when I'm next at leisure.

LXIV
They went to the Ridotto ('tis a place
  To which I mean to go myself to-morrow,
Just to divert my thoughts a little space
  Because I'm rather hippish, and may borrow
Some spirits, guessing at what kind of face
  May lurk beneath each mask; and as my sorrow
Slackens its pace sometimes, I'll make, or find,
Something shall leave it half an hour behind.)

LXV
Now Laura moves along the joyous crowd,
  Smiles in her eyes, and simpers on her lips;
To some she whispers, others speaks aloud;
  To some she curtsies, and to some she dips,
Complains of warmth, and this complaint avowed,
  Her lover brings the lemonade, she sips;
She then surveys, condemns, but pities still
Her dearest friends for being dressed so ill.

LXVI

One has false curls, another too much paint,
  A third—where did she buy that frightful turban?
A fourth's so pale she fears she's going to faint,
  A fifth's look's vulgar, dowdyish, and suburban,
A sixth's white silk has got a yellow taint,
  A seventh's thin muslin surely will be her bane,
And lo! an eighth appears,—'I'll see no more!'
For fear, like Banquo's kings, they reach a score.

LXVII

Meantime, while she was thus at others gazing,
  Others were levelling their looks at her;
She heard the men's half-whispered mode of praising,
  And, till 'twas done, determined not to stir;
The women only thought it quite amazing
  That, at her time of life, so many were
Admirers still,—but men are so debased,
Those brazen creatures always suit their taste.

LXVIII

For my part, now, I ne'er could understand
  Why naughty women—but I won't discuss
A thing which is a scandal to the land,
  I only don't see why it should be thus;
And if I were but in a gown and band,
  Just to entitle me to make a fuss,
I'd preach on this till Wilberforce and Romilly
Should quote in their next speeches from my homily.

LXIX

While Laura thus was seen, and seeing, smiling,
  Talking, she knew not why, and cared not what,
So that her female friends, with envy broiling,
  Beheld her airs and triumph, and all that;

And well-dressed males still kept before her filing,
    And passing bowed and mingled with her chat;
More than the rest one person seemed to stare
With pertinacity that's rather rare.

LXX

He was a Turk, the colour of mahogany;
    And Laura saw him, and at first was glad,
Because the Turks so much admire philogyny,
    Although their usage of their wives is sad;
'Tis said they use no better than a dog any
    Poor woman, whom they purchase like a pad:
They have a number, though they ne'er exhibit 'em,
Four wives by law, and concubines 'ad libitum.'

LXXI

They lock them up, and veil, and guard them daily,
    They scarcely can behold their male relations,
So that their moments do not pass so gaily
    As is supposed the case with northern nations;
Confinement, too, must make them look quite palely;
    And as the Turks abhor long conversations,
Their days are either passed in doing nothing,
Or bathing, nursing, making love, and clothing.

LXXII

They cannot read, and so don't lisp in criticism;
    Nor write, and so they don't affect the muse;
Were never caught in epigram or witticism,
    Have no romances, sermons, plays, reviews,—
In harams learning soon would make a pretty schism,
    But luckily these beauties are no 'Blues;'
No bustling Botherbys have they to show 'em
'That charming passage in the last new poem:'

No solemn, antique gentleman of rhyme,
  Who having angled all his life for fame,
And getting but a nibble at a time,
  Still fussily keeps fishing on, the same
Small 'Triton of the minnows,' the sublime
  Of mediocrity, the furious tame,
The echo's echo, usher of the school
Of female wits, boy bards—in short, a fool!

LXXIV

A stalking oracle of awful phrase,
  The approving 'Good!' (by no means GOOD in law)
Humming like flies around the newest blaze,
  The bluest of bluebottles you e'er saw,
Teasing with blame, excruciating with praise,
  Gorging the little fame he gets all raw,
Translating tongues he knows not even by letter,
And sweating plays so middling, bad were better.

LXXV

One hates an author that's *all author*, fellows
  In foolscap uniforms turned up with ink,
So very anxious, clever, fine, and jealous,
  One don't know what to say to them, or think,
Unless to puff them with a pair of bellows;
  Of coxcombry's worst coxcombs e'en the pink
Are preferable to these shreds of paper,
These unquenched snuffings of the midnight taper.

LXXVI

Of these same we see several, and of others,
  Men of the world, who know the world like men,
Scott, Rogers, Moore, and all the better brothers,
  Who think of something else besides the pen;

[61]

But for the children of the 'mighty mother's,'
　　The would-be wits, and can't-be gentlemen,
I leave them to their daily 'tea is ready,'
Smug coterie, and literary lady.

LXXVII

The poor dear Mussulwomen whom I mention
　　Have none of these instructive pleasant people,
And *one* would seem to them a new invention,
　　Unknown as bells within a Turkish steeple;
I think 'twould almost be worth while to pension
　　(Though best-sown projects very often reap ill)
A missionary author, just to preach
Our Christian usage of the parts of speech.

LXXVIII

No chemistry for them unfolds her gases,
　　No metaphysics are let loose in lectures,
No circulating library amasses
　　Religious novels, moral tales, and strictures
Upon the living manners, as they pass us;
　　No exhibition glares with annual pictures;
They stare not on the stars from out their attics,
Nor deal (thank God for that!) in mathematics.

LXXIX

Why I thank God for that is no great matter,
　　I have my reasons, you no doubt suppose,
And as, perhaps, they would not highly flatter,
　　I'll keep them for my life (to come) in prose;
I fear I have a little turn for satire,
　　And yet methinks the older that one grows
Inclines us more to laugh than scold, though laughter
Leaves us so doubly serious shortly after.

LXXX

Oh, mirth and innocence! Oh, milk and water!
  Ye happy mixtures of more happy days!
In these sad centuries of sin and slaughter,
  Abominable Man no more allays
His thirst with such pure beverage. No matter,
  I love you both, and both shall have my praise:
Oh, for old Saturn's reign of sugar-candy!—
Meantime I drink to your return in brandy.

LXXXI

Our Laura's Turk still kept his eyes upon her,
  Less in the Mussulman than Christian way,
Which seems to say, 'Madam, I do you honour,
  'And while I please to stare, you'll please to stay.
Could staring win a woman, this had won her,
  But Laura could not thus be led astray;
She had stood fire too long and well, to boggle
Even at this stranger's most outlandish ogle.

LXXXII

The morning now was on the point of breaking,
  A turn of time at which I would advise
Ladies who have been dancing, or partaking
  In any other kind of exercise,
To make their preparations for forsaking
  The ball-room ere the sun begins to rise,
Because when once the lamps and candles fail,
His blushes make them look a little pale.

LXXXIII

I've seen some balls and revels in my time,
  And stayed them over for some silly reason,
And then I looked (I hope it was no crime)
  To see what lady best stood out the season;

And though I've seen some thousands in their prime,
  Lovely and pleasing, and who still may please on,
I never saw but one (the stars withdrawn)
Whose bloom could after dancing dare the dawn.

LXXXIV

The name of this Aurora I'll not mention,
  Although I might, for she was nought to me
More than that patent work of God's invention,
  A charming woman, whom we like to see;
But writing names would merit reprehension,
  Yet if you like to find out this fair *she*,
At the next London or Parisian ball
You still may mark her cheek, out-blooming all.

LXXXV

Laura, who knew it would not do at all
  To meet the daylight after seven hours' sitting
Among three thousand people at a ball,
  To make her curtsy thought it right and fitting;
The Count was at her elbow with her shawl,
  And they the room were on the point of quitting,
When lo! those cursed gondoliers had got
Just in the very place where they *should not*.

LXXXVI

In this they're like our coachmen, and the cause
  Is much the same—the crowd, and pulling, hauling,
With blasphemies enough to break their jaws,
  They make a never intermitted bawling.
At home, our Bow-street gemmem keep the laws,
  And here a sentry stands within your calling;
But for all that, there is a deal of swearing,
And nauseous words past mentioning or bearing.

[64]

LXXXVII

The Count and Laura found their boat at last,
  And homeward floated o'er the silent tide,
Discussing all the dances gone and past;
  The dancers and their dresses, too, besides;
Some little scandals eke; but all aghast
  (As to their palace-stairs the rowers glide)
Sate Laura by the side of her Adorer,
When lo! the Mussulman was there before her.

LXXXVIII

'Sir,' said the Count, with brow exceeding grave,
  'Your unexpected presence here will make
It necessary for myself to crave
  Its import? But perhaps 'tis a mistake;
I hope it is so; and, at once to waive
  All compliment, I hope so for *your* sake;
You understand my meaning, or you *shall*.'
'Sir,' (quoth the Turk) ' 'tis no mistake at all:

LXXXIX

'That lady is *my wife!*' Much wonder paints
  The lady's changing cheek, as well it might;
But where an Englishwoman sometimes faints,
  Italian females don't do so outright;
They only call a little on their saints,
  And then come to themselves, almost or quite;
Which saves much hartshorn, salts, and sprinkling faces
And cutting stays, as usual in such cases.

XC

She said,—what could she say? Why, not a word:
  But the Count courteously invited in
The stranger, much appeased by what he heard:
  'Such things, perhaps, we'd best discuss within,'

[65]

Said he; 'don't let us make ourselves absurd
  In public, by a scene, nor raise a din,
For then the chief and only satisfaction
Will be much quizzing on the whole transaction.'

XCI

They entered, and for coffee called—it came,
  A beverage for Turks and Christians both,
Although the way they make it's not the same.
  Now Laura, much recovered, or less loth
To speak, cries 'Beppo! what's your pagan name?
  Bless me! your beard is of amazing growth!
And how came you to keep away so long?
Are you not sensible 'twas very wrong?

XCII

'And are you *really, truly*, now a Turk?
  With any other women did you wive?
Is't true they use their fingers for a fork?
  Well, that's the prettiest shawl—as I'm alive!
You'll give it me? They say you eat no pork.
  And how so many years did you contrive
To—bless me! did I ever? No, I never
Saw a man grown so yellow! How's your liver?

XCIII

'Beppo! that beard of yours becomes you not;
  It shall be shaved before you're a day older:
Why do you wear it? Oh! I had forgot—
  Pray don't you think the weather here is colder?
How do I look? You shan't stir from this spot
  In that queer dress, for fear that some beholder
Should find you out, and make the story known.
How short your hair is! Lord! how grey it's grown!'

[66]

What answer Beppo made to these demands
　Is more than I know. He was cast away
About where Troy stood once, and nothing stands;
　Became a slave of course, and for his pay
Had bread and bastinadoes, till some bands
　Of pirates landing in a neighbouring bay,
He joined the rogues and prospered, and became
A renegado of indifferent fame.

But he grew rich, and with his riches grew so
　Keen the desire to see his home again,
He thought himself in duty bound to do so,
　And not be always thieving on the main;
Lonely he felt, at times, as Robin Crusoe,
　And so he hired a vessel come from Spain,
Bound for Corfu: she was a fine polacca,
Manned with twelve hands, and laden with tobacco.

Himself, and much (heaven knows how gotten!) cash,
　He then embarked, with risk of life and limb,
And got clear off, although the attempt was rash;
　He said that *Providence* protected him—
For my part, I say nothing—lest we clash
　In our opinions:—well, the ship was trim,
Set sail, and kept her reckoning fairly on,
Except three days of calm when off Cape Bonn.

They reached the island, he transferred his lading,
　And self and livestock to another bottom,
And passed for a true Turkey-merchant, trading
　With goods of various names, but I've forgot 'em.

However, he got off by this evading,
   Or else the people would perhaps have shot him;
And thus at Venice landed to reclaim
His wife, religion, house, and Christian name.

His wife received, the patriarch re-baptised him,
   (He made the church a present, by the way;)
He then threw off the garments which disguised him,
   And borrowed the Count's smallclothes for a day:
His friends the more for his long absence prized him,
   Finding he'd wherewithal to make them gay,
With dinners, where he oft became the laugh of them,
For stories—but *I* don't believe the half of them.

Whate'er his youth had suffered, his old age
   With wealth and talking made him some amends;
Though Laura sometimes put him in a rage,
   I've heard the Count and he were always friends.
My pen is at the bottom of a page,
   Which being finished, here the story ends;
'Tis to be wished it had been sooner done,
But stories somehow lengthen when begun.

The Vision of Judgment

PREFACE

It hath been wisely said, that 'One fool makes many'; and
it hath been poetically observed—

   '*That fools rush in where angels fear to tread.*' POPE

If Mr. Southey had not rushed in where he had no business,

[68]

and where he never was before, and never will be again, the following poem would not have been written. It is not impossible that it may be as good as his own, seeing that it cannot, by any species of stupidity, natural or acquired, be *worse*. The gross flattery, the dull impudence, the renegado intolerance, and impious cant, of the poem by the author of 'Wat Tyler,' are something so stupendous as to form the sublime of himself—containing the quintessence of his own attributes.

So much for his poem—a word on his preface. In this preface it has pleased the magnanimous Laureate to draw the picture of a supposed 'Satanic School,' the which he doth recommend to the notice of the legislature; thereby adding to his other laurels the ambition of those of an informer. If there exists anywhere, except in his imagination, such a School, is he not sufficiently armed against it by his own intense vanity? The truth is that there are certain writers whom Mr. S. imagine, like Scrub, to have 'talked of *him*; for they laughed consumedly.'

I think I know enough of most of the writers to whom he is supposed to allude, to assert, that they, in their individual capacities, have done more good, in the charities of life, to their fellow-creatures, in any one year, than Mr. Southey has done harm to himself by his absurdities in his whole life; and this is saying a great deal. But I have a few questions to ask.

1stly, Is Mr. Southey the author of 'Wat Tyler?'

2ndly, Was he not refused a remedy at law by the highest judge of his beloved England, because it was a blasphemous and seditious publication?

3rdly, Was he not entitled by William Smith, in full parliament, 'a rancorous renegado?'

4thly, Is he not poet laureate, with his own lines on Martin the regicide staring him in the face?

And, 5thly, Putting the four preceding items together,

[69]

with what conscience dare *he* call the attention of the laws to the publications of others, be they what they may?

I say nothing of the cowardice of such a proceeding; its meanness speaks for itself; but I wish to touch upon the *motive*, which is neither more nor less than that Mr. S. has been laughed at a little in some recent publications, as he was of yore in the 'Anti-jacobin,' by his present patrons. Hence all this 'skimble scamble stuff' about 'Satanic,' and so forth. However, it is worthy of him— '*qualis ab incepto.*'

If there is anything obnoxious to the political opinions of a portion of the public in the following poem, they may thank Mr. Southey. He might have written hexameters, as he has written everything else, for aught that the writer cared—had they been upon another subject. But to attempt to canonise a monarch, who, whatever were his household virtues, was neither a successful nor a patriot king,—inasmuch as several years of his reign passed in war with America and Ireland, to say nothing of the aggression upon France—like all other exaggeration, necessarily begets opposition. In whatever manner he may be spoken of in this new 'Vision,' his *public* career will not be more favourably transmitted by history. Of his private virtues (although a little expensive to the nation) there can be no doubt.

With regard to the supernatural personages treated of, I can only say that I know as much about them, and (as an honest man) have a better right to talk of them than Robert Southey. I have also treated them more tolerantly. The way in which that poor insane creature, the Laureate, deals about his judgments in the next world, is like his own judgment in this. If it was not completely ludicrous, it would be something worse. I don't think that there is much more to say at present.

QUEVEDO REDIVIVUS

P.S.—It is possible that some readers may object, in these objectionable times, to the freedom with which saints, angels, and spiritual persons discourse in this 'Vision'. But, for precedents upon such points, I must refer him to Fielding's 'Journey from this World to the next,' and to the Visions of myself, the said Quevedo, in Spanish or translated. The reader is also requested to observe, that no doctrinal tenets are insisted upon or discussed; that the person of the Deity is carefully withheld from sight, which is more than can be said for the Laureate, who hath thought proper to make him talk, not 'like a school-divine,' but like the unscholarlike Mr. Southey. The whole action passes on the outside of heaven: and Chaucer's 'Wife of Bath,' Pulci's 'Morgante Maggiore,' Swift's 'Tale of a Tub,' and the other works above referred to, are cases in point of the freedom with which saints, &c. may be permitted to converse in works not intended to be serious.

Q.R.

*** Mr. Southey being, as he says, a good Christian and vindictive, threatens, I understand, a reply to this our answer. It is to be hoped that his visionary faculties will in the meantime have acquired a little more judgment, properly so called: otherwise he will get him self into new dilemmas. These apostate jacobins furnish rich rejoinders. Let him take a specimen. Mr. Southey laudeth grievously 'one Mr. Landor,' who cultivates much private renown in the shape of Latin verses; and not long ago, the poet laureate dedicated to him, it appeareth, one of his fugitive lyrics, upon the strength of a poem called '*Gebir*.' Who could suppose, that in this same Gebir the aforesaid Savage Landor (for such is his grim cognomen) putteth into the infernal regions no less a person that the hero of his friend Mr. Southey's heaven,—yea, even George the

Third! See also how personal Savage becometh, when he hath a mind. The following is his portrait of our late gracious sovereign:

(*Prince Gebir having descended into the infernal regions, the shades of his royal ancestors are, at his request, called up to his view; and he exclaims to his ghostly guide*)

> 'Aroar, what wretch that nearest us? what wretch
> Is that with eyebrows white and slanting brow?
> Listen! him yonder who, bound down supine,
> Shrinks yelling from that sword there, engine-hung.
> He too amongst my ancestors! I hate
> The despot, but the dastard I despise.
> Was he our countryman?'
>   'Alas, O king!
> Iberia bore him, but the breed accurst
> Inclement winds blew blighting from north-east'.
> 'He was a warrior then, nor fear'd the gods?'
> 'Gebir, he fear'd the demons, not the gods,
> Though them indeed his daily face adored;
> And was no warrior, yet the thousand lives
> Squander'd, as stones to exercise a sling,
> And the tame cruelty and cold caprice—
> Oh madness of mankind! address'd, adored!'
>   *Gebir*, p. 28

I omit noticing some edifying Ithyphallics of Savagius, wishing to keep the proper veil over them, if his grave but somewhat indiscreet worshipper will suffer it; but certainly these teachers of 'great moral lessons' are apt to be found in strange company.

Southey succeeded Pye as poet laureate in 1813, and promply switched political allegiances, from liberalism to an outright support of monarchic dealings. Southey's own *Vision of Judgment* contained an attack on Byron in its Preface, melo-dramatising Byron as the founder of a 'Satanic school' of poetry. The rest of the poem, written in 1820 after the death of George III, praised the monarch. Byron's umbrage was therefore personal and political, although in 1813, Byron had described Southey in a letter as 'the only entire man of letters'. But then there had been a time when he liked Wordsworth, too.

Landor's *Gebir* was published in 1798. I have yet to meet someone who's read it.

THE VISION OF JUDGMENT

I

Saint Peter sat by the celestial gate:
  His keys were rusty, and the lock was dull,
So little trouble had been given of late;
  Not that the place by any means was full,
But since the Gallic era 'eighty-eight'
  The devils had ta'en a longer, stronger pull,
And 'a pull altogether,' as they say
At sea—which drew most souls another way.

II

The angels all were singing out of tune,
  And hoarse with having little else to do,
Excepting to wind up the sun and moon,
  Or curb a runaway young star or two,
Or wild colt of a comet, which too soon
  Broke out of bounds o'er the ethereal blue,
Splitting some planet with its playful tail,
As boats are sometimes by a wanton whale.

III

The guardian seraphs had retired on high,
  Finding their charges past all care below;
Terrestrial business filled nought in the sky
  Save the recording angel's black bureau;

Who found, indeed, the facts to multiply
    With such rapidity of vice and woe,
That he had stripped off both his wings in quills,
And yet was in arrear of human ills.

IV

His business so augmented of late years,
    That he was forced, against his will no doubt,
(Just like those cherubs, earthly ministers,)
    For some resource to turn himself about,
And claim the help of his celestial peers,
    To aid him ere he should be quite worn out
By the increased demand for his remarks:
Six angels and twelve saints were named his clerks.

V

This was a handsome board—at least for heaven;
    And yet they had even then enough to do,
So many conquerors' cars were daily driven,
    So many kingdoms fitted up anew;
Each day too slew its thousands six or seven,
    Till at the crowning carnage, Waterloo,
They threw their pens down in divine disgust—
The page was so besmeared with blood and dust.

VI

This by the way; 'tis not mine to record
    What angels shrink from: even the very devil
On this occasion his own work abhorred,
    So surfeited with the infernal revel:
Though he himself had sharpened every sword,
    It almost quenched his innate thirst of evil.
(Here Satan's sole good work deserves insertion—
'Tis, that he has both generals in reversion.)

[74]

VII

Let's skip a few short years of hollow peace,
　Which peopled earth no better, hell as wont,
And heaven none—they form the tyrant's lease,
　With nothing but new names subscribed upon't;
'Twill one day finish: meantime they increase,
　'With seven heads and ten horns,' and all in front,
Like Saint John's foretold beast; but ours are born
Less formidable in the head than horn.

VIII

In the first year of freedom's second dawn
　Died George the Third; although no tyrant, one
Who shielded tyrants, till each sense withdrawn
　Left him nor mental nor external sun:
A better farmer ne'er brushed dew from lawn,
　A worse king never left a realm undone!
He died—but left his subjects still behind,
One half as mad—and t'other no less blind.

IX

He died! his death made no great stir on earth:
　His burial made some pomp; there was profusion
Of velvet, gilding, brass, and no great dearth
　Of aught but tears—save those shed by collusion.
For these things may be bought at their true worth;
　Of elegy there was the due infusion—
Bought also; and the torches, cloaks and banners,
Heralds, and relics of old Gothic manners,

X

Formed a sepulchral melodrame. Of all
　The fools who flocked to swell or see the show,
Who cared about the corpse? The funeral
　Made the attraction, and the black the woe.

There throbbed not there a thought which pierced the pall;
   And when the gorgeous coffin was laid low,
It seemed the mockery of hell to fold
The rottenness of eighty years in gold.

XI

So mix his body with the dust! It might
   Return to what it *must* far sooner, were
The natural compound left alone to fight
   Its way back into earth, and fire, and air;
But the unnatural balsams merely blight
   What nature made him at his birth, as bare
As the mere million's base unmummied clay—
Yet all his spices but prolong decay.

XII

He's dead—and upper earth with him has done;
   He's buried; save the undertaker's bill,
Or lapidary scrawl, the world is gone
   For him, unless he left a German will:
But where's the proctor who will ask his son?
   In whom his qualities are reigning still,
Except that household virtue, most uncommon,
Of constancy to a bad, ugly woman.

XIII

'God save the king!' It is a large economy
   In God to save the like; but if he will
Be saving, all the better; for not one am I
   Of those who think damnation better still:
I hardly know too if not quite alone am I
   In this small hope of bettering future ill
By circumscribing, with some slight restriction,
The eternity of hell's hot jurisdiction.

XIV

I know this is unpopular; I know
   'Tis blasphemous; I know one may be damned
For hoping no one else may e'er be so;
   I know my catechism; I know we're crammed
With the best doctrines till we quite o'erflow;
   I know that all save England's church have shammed,
And that the other twice two hundred churches
And synagogues have made a *damned* bad purchase.

XV

God help us all! God help me too! I am
   God knows, as helpless as the devil can wish,
And not a whit more difficult to damn,
   Than is to bring to land a late-hooked fish,
Or to the butcher to purvey the lamb;
   Not that I'm fit for such a noble dish,
As one day will be that immortal fry
Of almost every body born to die.

XVI

Saint Peter sat by the celestial gate,
   And nodded o'er his keys: when, lo! there came
A wondrous noise he had not heard of late—
   A rushing sound of wind, and stream, and flame;
In short, a roar of things extremely great,
   Which would have made aught save a saint exclaim;
But he, with first a start and then a wink,
Said, 'There's another star gone out, I think!'

XVII

But ere he could return to his repose,
   A cherub flapped his right wing o'er his eyes—
At which Saint Peter yawned, and rubbed his nose:
   'Saint porter,' said the angel, 'prithee rise!'

[77]

Waving a goodly wing, which glowed, as glows
  An earthly peacock's tail, with heavenly dyes:
To which the saint replied, 'Well, what's the matter?
'Is Lucifer come back with all this clatter?'

XVIII

'No,' quoth the cherub: 'George the Third is dead.'
  'And who *is* George the Third?' repled the apostle:
'*What George? what Third?*' 'The king of England,' said
  The angel. 'Well! he won't find kings to jostle
Him on his way; but does he wear his head?
  Because the last we saw here had a tustle,
And ne'er would have got into heaven's good graces,
Had he not flung his head in all our faces.

XIX

'He was, if I remember, king of France;
  That head of his, which could not keep a crown
On earth, yet ventured in my face to advance
  A claim to those of martyrs—like my own:
If I had had my sword, as I had once
  When I cut ears off, I had cut him down;
But having but my *keys*, and not my brand,
I only knocked his head from out his hand.

XX

'And then he set up such a headless howl,
  That all the saints came out and took him in;
And there he sits by St. Paul, cheek by jowl;
  That fellow Paul—the parvenù! The skin
Of Saint Bartholomew, which makes his cowl
  In heaven, and upon earth redeemed his sin,
So as to make a martyr, never sped
Better than did this weak and wooden head.

[78]

XXI

'But had it come up here upon its shoulders,
  There would have been a different tale to tell:
The fellow-feeling in the saint's beholders
  Seems to have acted on them like a spell;
And so this very foolish head heaven solders
  Back on its trunk: it may be very well,
And seems the custom here to overthrow
Whatever has been wisely done below.'

The angel answered, 'Peter! do not pout:
  The king who comes has head and all entire,
And never knew much what it was about—
  He did as doth the puppet—by its wire,
And will be judged like all the rest, no doubt:
  My business and your own is not to inquire
Into such matters, but to mind our cue—
Which is to act as we are bid to do.'

XXIII

While thus they spake, the angelic caravan,
  Arriving like a rush of mighty wind,
Cleaving the fields of space, as doth the swan
  Some silver stream (say Ganges, Nile, or Inde,
Or Thames, or Tweed), and midst them an old man
  With an old soul, and both extremely blind,
Halted before the gate, and in his shroud
Seated their fellow-traveller on a cloud.

But bringing up the rear of this bright host
  A Spirit of a different aspect waved
His wings, like thunder-clouds above some coast
  Whose barren beach with frequent wrecks is paved;

His brow was like the deep when tempest-tossed;
  Fierce and unfathomable thoughts engraved
Eternal wrath on his immortal face,
And *where* he gazed a gloom pervaded space.

XXV

As he drew near, he gazed upon the gate
  Ne'er to be entered more by him or Sin,
With such a glance of supernatural hate,
  As made Saint Peter wish himself within;
He pattered with his keys at a great rate,
  And sweated through his apostolic skin:
Of course his perspiration was but ichor,
Or some such other spiritual liquor.

XXVI

The very cherubs huddled all together,
  Like birds when soars the falcon; and they felt
A tingling to the tip of every feather,
  And formed a circle like Orion's belt
Around their poor old charge; who scarce knew whither
  His guards had led him, though they gently dealt
With royal manes (for by many stories,
And true, we learn the angels all are Tories).

XXVII

As things were in this posture, the gate flew
  Asunder, and the flashing of its hinges
Flung over space an universal hue
  Of many-coloured flame, until its tinges
Reached even our speck of earth, and made a new
  Aurora borealis spread its fringes
O'er the North Pole; the same seen, when ice-bound,
By Captain Parry's crew, in 'Melville's Sound.'

XXVIII

And from the gate thrown open issued beaming
  A beautiful and mighty Thing of light,
Radiant with glory, like a banner streaming
  Victorious from some world-o'erthrowing fight:
My poor comparisons must needs be teeming
  With earthly likenesses, for here the night
Of clay obscures our best conceptions, saving
Johanna Southcote, or Bob Southey raving.

'Twas the archangel Michael; all men know
  The make of angels and archangels, since
There's scarce a scribbler has not one to show,
  From the fiends' leader to the angels' prince;
There also are some altar-pieces, though
  I really can't say that they much evince
One's inner notions of immortal spirits;
But let the connoisseurs explain *their* merits.

XXX

Michael flew forth in glory and in good;
  A goodly work of him from whom all glory
And good arise; the portal past—he stood;
  Before him the young cherubs and saints hoary
(I say *young*, begging to be understood
  By looks, not years; and should be very sorry
To state, they were not older than St. Peter,
But merely that they seemed a little sweeter).

The cherubs and the saints bowed down before
  That arch-angelic hierarch, the first
Of essences angelical who wore
  The aspect of a god; but this ne'er nursed

Pride in his heavenly bosom, in whose core
    No thought, save for his Maker's service, durst
Intrude, however glorified and high;
He knew him but the viceroy of the sky.

XXXII

He and the sombre, silent Spirit met—
    They knew each other both for good and ill;
Such was their power, that neither could forget
    His former friend and future foe; but still
There was a high, immortal, proud regret
    In either's eye, as if 'twere less their will
Than destiny to make the eternal years
Their date of war, and their 'champ clos' the spheres.

XXXIII

But here they were in neutral space: we know
    From Job, that Satan hath the power to pay
A heavenly visit thrice a year or so;
    And that the 'sons of God,' like those of clay,
Must keep him company; and we might show
    From the same book, in how polite a way
The dialogue is held between the Powers
Of Good and Evil—but 'twould take up hours.

XXXIV

And this is not a theologic tract,
    To prove with Hebrew and with Arabic,
If Job be allegory or a fact,
    But a true narrative; and thus I pick
From out the whole but such and such an act
    As sets aside the slightest thought of trick.
'Tis every tittle true, beyond suspicion,
And accurate as any other vision.

XXXV

The spirits were in neutral space, before
  The gate of heaven; like eastern thresholds is
The place where Death's grand cause is argued o'er,
  And souls despatched to that world or to this;
And therefore Michael and the other wore
  A civil aspect: though they did not kiss,
Yet still between his Darkness and his Brightness
There passed a mutual glance of great politeness.

XXXVI

The Archangel bowed, not like a modern beau,
  But with a graceful oriental bend,
Pressing one radiant arm just where below
  The heart in good men is supposed to tend;
He turned as to an equal, not too low,
  But kindly; Satan met his ancient friend
With more hauteur, as might an old Castilian
Poor noble meet a mushroom rich civilian.

XXXVII

He merely bent his diabolic brow
  An instant; and then raising it, he stood
In act to assert his right or wrong, and show
  Cause why King George by no means could or should
Make out a case to be exempt from woe
  Eternal, more than other kings, endued
With better sense and hearts, whom history mentions,
Who long have 'paved hell with their good intentions.'

XXXVIII

Michael began: 'What wouldst thou with this man,
  Now dead, and brought before the Lord? What ill
Hath he wrought since his mortal race began,
  That thou canst claim him? Speak! and do thy will,

If it be just: if in this earthly span
  He hath been greatly failing to fulfil
His duties as a king and mortal, say,
And he is thine; if not, let him have way.'

XXXIX

'Michael!' replied the Prince of Air, 'even here,
  Before the Gate of him thou servest, must
I claim my subject: and will make appear
  That as he was my worshipper in dust,
So shall he be in spirit, although dear
  To thee and thine, because nor wine nor lust
Were of his weaknesses; yet on the throne
He reigned o'er millions to serve me alone.

XL

'Look to *our* earth, or rather *mine*; it was,
  Once, more thy master's: but I triumph not
In this poor planet's conquest; nor, alas!
  Need he thou servest envy me my lot:
With all the myriads of bright worlds which pass
  In worship round him, he may have forgot
Yon weak creation of such paltry things:
I think few worth damnation save their kings,

XLI

'And these but as a kind of quit-rent, to
  Assert my right as lord: and even had
I such an inclination, 'twere (as you
  Well know) superfluous; they are grown so bad,
That hell has nothing better left to do
  Than leave them to themselves: so much more mad
And evil by their own internal curse,
Heaven cannot make them better, nor I worse.

[84]

XLII

'Look to the earth, I said, and say again:
  When this old, blind, mad, helpless, weak, poor worm
Began in youth's first bloom and flush to reign,
  The world and he both wore a different form,
And much of earth and all the watery plain
  Of ocean called him king: through many a storm
His isles had floated on the abyss of time;
For the rough virtues chose them for their clime.

XLIII

'He came to his sceptre young; he leaves it old:
  Look to the state in which he found his realm,
And left it; and his annals too behold,
  How to a minion first he gave the helm;
How grew upon his heart a thirst for gold,
  The beggar's vice, which can but overwhelm
The meanest hearts; and for the rest, but glance
Thine eye along America and France.

XLIV

' 'Tis true, he was a tool from first to last
  (I have the workmen safe); but as a tool
So let him be consumed. From out the past
  Of ages, since mankind have known the rule
Of monarchs—from the bloody rolls amassed
  Of sin and slaughter—from the Caesar's school,
Take the worst pupil; and produce a reign
More drenched with gore, more cumbered with the slain.

XLV

'He ever warred with freedom and the free:
  Nations as men, home subjects, foreign foes,
So that they uttered the word "Liberty!"
  Found George the Third their first opponent. Whose

[85]

History was ever stained as his will be
    With national and individual woes?
I grant his household abstinence; I grant
His neutral virtues, which most monarchs want;

XLVI

'I know he was a constant consort; own
    He was a decent sire, and middling lord.
All this is much, and most upon a throne;
    As temperance, if at Apicius' board,
Is more than at an anchorite's supper shown.
    I grant him all the kindest can accord;
And this was well for him, but not for those
Millions who found him what oppression chose.

XLVII

'The New World shook him off; the Old yet groans
    Beneath what he and his prepared, if not
Completed: he leaves heirs on many thrones
    To all his vices, without what begot
Compassion for him—his tame virtues, drones
    Who sleep, or despots who have now forgot
A lesson which shall be re-taught them, wake
Upon the thrones of earth; but let them quake!

XLVIII

'Five millions of the primitive, who hold
    The faith which makes ye great on earth, implored
A *part* of that vast *all* they held of old,—
    Freedom to worship—not alone your Lord,
Michael, but you, and you, Saint Peter! Cold
    Must be your souls, if you have not abhorred
The foe to Catholic participation
In all the license of a Christian nation.

[86]

XLIX

'True! he allowed them to pray God; but as
  A consequence of prayer, refused the law
Which would have placed them upon the same base
  With those who did not hold the saints in awe.'
But here Saint Peter started from his place,
  And cried, 'You may the prisoner withdraw:
Ere heaven shall ope her portals to this Guelph,
While I am guard, may I be damned myself!

L

'Sooner will I with Cerberus exchange
  My office (and *his* is no sinecure)
Than see this royal Bedlam bigot range
  The azure fields of heaven, of that be sure!'
'Saint!' replied Satan, 'you do well to avenge
  The wrongs he made your satellites endure;
And if to this exchange you should be given,
I'll try to coax *our* Cerberus up to heaven!'

LI

Here Michael interposed: 'Good saint! and devil!
  Pray, not so fast; you both outrun discretion.
Saint Peter! you were wont to be more civil:
  Satan! excuse this warmth of his expression,
And condescension to the vulgar's level:
  Even saints sometimes forget themselves in session.
Have you got more to say?'—'No.'—'If you please,
I'll trouble you to call your witnesses.'

LII

Then Satan turned and waved his swarthy hand,
  Which stirred with its electric qualities
Clouds farther off than we can understand,
  Although we find him sometimes in our skies;

[87]

Infernal thunder shook both sea and land
  In all the planets, and hell's batteries
Let off the artillery, which Milton mentions
As one of Satan's most sublime inventions.

LIII

This was a signal unto such damned souls
  As have the privilege of their damnation
Extended far beyond the mere controls
  Of worlds past, present, or to come; no station
Is theirs particularly in the rolls
  Of hell assigned; but where their inclination
Or business carries them in search of game,
They may range freely—being damned the same.

LIV

They are proud of this—as very well they may,
  It being a sort of knighthood, or gilt key
Stuck in their loins; or like to an 'entré'
  Up the back stairs, or such free-masonry.
I borrow my comparisons from clay,
  Being clay myself. Let not those spirits be
Offended with such base low likenesses;
We know their posts are nobler far than these.

LV

When the great signal ran from heaven to hell—
  About ten million times the distance reckoned
From our sun to its earth, as we can tell
  How much time it takes up, even to a second,
For every ray that travels to dispel
  The fogs of London, through which, dimly beaconed,
The weathercocks are gilt some thrice a year,
If that the *summer* is not too severe:

[88]

I say that I can tell—'twas half a minute;
  I know the solar beams take up more time
Ere, packed up for their journey, they begin it;
  But then their telegraph is less sublime,
And if they ran a race, they would not win it
  'Gainst Satan's couriers bound for their own clime.
The sun takes up some years for every ray
To reach its goal—the devil not half a day.

Upon the verge of space, about the size
  Of half-a-crown, a little speck appeared
(I've seen a something like it in the skies
  In the Aegean, ere a squall); it neared,
And, growing bigger, took another guise;
  Like an aërial ship it tacked, and steered,
Or *was* steered (I am doubtful of the grammar
Of the last phrase, which makes the stanza stammer;—

But take your choice): and then it grew a cloud;
  And so it was—a cloud of witnesses.
But such a cloud! No land ere saw a crowd
  Of locusts numerous as the heavens saw these;
They shadowed with their myriads space; their loud
  And varied cries were like those of wild geese
(If nations may be likened to a goose),
And realised the phrase of 'hell broke loose.'

Here crashed a sturdy oath of stout John Bull,
  Who damned away his eyes as heretofore:
There Paddy brogued 'By Jasus!'—'What's your wull?'
  The temperate Scot exclaimed: the French ghost swore

In certain terms I shan't translate in full,
    As the first coachman will; and 'midst the war,
The voice of Jonathan was heard to express,
'*Our* president is going to war, I guess.'

LX

Besides there were the Spaniard, Dutch, and Dane;
    In short, an universal shoal of shades
From Otaheite's isle to Salisbury Plain,
    Of all climes and professions, years and trades,
Ready to swear against the good king's reign,
    Bitter as clubs in cards are against spades:
All summoned by this grand 'subpœna,' to
Try if kings mayn't be damned like me or you.

LXI

When Michael saw this host, he first grew pale,
    As angels can; next, like Italian twilight,
He turned all colours—as a peacock's tail,
    Or sunset streaming through a Gothic skylight
In some old abbey, or a trout not stale,
    Or distant lightning on the horizon *by* night,
Or a fresh rainbow, or a grand review
Of thirty regiments in red, green, and blue.

LXII

Then he addressed himself to Satan: 'Why—
    My good old friend, for such I deem you, though
Our different parties make us fight so shy,
    I ne'er mistake you for a *personal* foe;
Our difference is *political*, and I
    Trust that, whatever may occur below,
You know my great respect for you: and this
Makes me regret whate'er you do amiss—

[90]

LXIII

'Why, my dear Lucifer, would you abuse
  My call for witnesses? I did not mean
That you should half of earth and hell produce;
  'Tis even superfluous, since two honest, clean,
True testimonies are enough: we lose
  Our time, nay, our eternity, between
The accusation and defence: if we
Hear both, 'twill stretch our immortality.'

LXIV

Satan replied, 'To me the matter is
  Indifferent, in a personal point of view:
I can have fifty better souls than this
  With far less trouble than we have gone through
Already; and I merely argued his
  Late majesty of Britain's case with you
Upon a point of form: you may dispose
Of him; I've kings enough below, God knows!'

LXV

Thus spoke the Demon (late called 'multifaced'
  By multo-scribbling Southey). 'Then we'll call
One or two persons of the myriads placed
  Around our congress, and dispense with all
The rest,' quoth Michael: 'Who may be so graced
  As to speak first? there's choice enough—who shall
It be?' Then Satan answered, 'There are many;
But you may choose Jack Wilkes as well as any.'

LXVI

A merry, cock-eyed, curious-looking sprite
  Upon the instant started from the throng,
Dressed in a fashion now forgotten quite;
  For all the fashions of the flesh stick long

By people in the next world; where unite
    All the costumes since Adam's, right or wrong,
From Eve's fig-leaf down to the petticoat,
Almost as scanty, of days less remote.

LXVII

The spirit looked around upon the crowds
    Assembled, and exclaimed, 'My friends of all
The spheres, we shall catch cold amongst these clouds;
    So let's to business: why this general call?
If those are freeholders I see in shrouds,
    And 'tis for an election that they bawl,
Behold a candidate with unturned coat!
Saint Peter, may I count upon your vote?

LXVIII

'Sir,' replied Michael, 'you mistake; these things
    Are of a former life, and what we do
Above is more august; to judge of kings
    Is the tribunal met: so now you know.'
'Then I presume those gentlemen with wings,'
    Said Wilkes, 'are cherubs; and that soul below
Looks much like George the Third, but to my mind
A good deal older—bless me! is he blind?'

LXIX

'He is what you behold him, and his doom
    Depends upon his deeds,' the Angel said;
'If you have aught to arraign in him, the tomb
    Gives license to the humblest beggar's head
To lift itself against the loftiest.'—'Some,'
    Said Wilkes, 'don't wait to see them laid in lead,
For such a liberty—and I, for one,
Have told them what I thought beneath the sun.'

LXX

'*Above* the sun repeat, then, what thou hast
 To urge against him,' said the Archangel. 'Why,'
Replied the spirit, 'since old scores are past,
 Must I turn evidence? In faith, not I.
Besides, I beat him hollow at the last,
 With all his Lords and Commons: in the sky
I don't like ripping up old stories, since
His conduct was but natural in a prince.

LXXI

'Foolish, no doubt, and wicked, to oppress
 A poor unlucky devil without a shilling;
But then I blame the man himself much less
 Than Bute and Grafton, and shall be unwilling
To see him punished here for their excess,
 Since they were both damned long ago, and still in
Their place below: for me, I have forgiven,
And vote his "habeas corpus" into heaven.'

LXXII

'Wilkes,' said the Devil, 'I understand all this;
 You turned to half a courtier ere you died,
And seem to think it would not be amiss
 To grow a whole one on the other side
Of Charon's ferry; you forget that *his*
 Reign is concluded; whatsoe'er betide,
He won't be sovereign more: you've lost your labour,
For at the best he will but be your neighbour.

LXXIII

'However, I knew what to think of it,
 When I beheld you in your jesting way,
Flitting and whispering round about the spit
 Where Belial, upon duty for the day,

[93]

With Fox's lard was basting William Pitt,
    His pupil; I knew what to think, I say:
That fellow even in hell breeds farther ills;
I'll have him *gagged*—'twas one of his own bills.

LXXIV

'Call Junius!' From the crowd a shadow stalked,
    And at the name there was a general squeeze,
So that the very ghosts no longer walked
    In comfort, at their own aërial ease,
But were all rammed, and jammed (but to be balked,
    As we shall see), and jostled hands and knees,
Like wind compressed and pent within a bladder,
Or like a human colic, which is sadder.

LXXV

The shadow came—a tall, thin, grey-haired figure,
    That looked as it had been a shade on earth;
Quick in its motions, with an air of vigour,
    But nought to mark its breeding or its birth;
Now it waxed little, then again grew bigger,
    With now an air of gloom, or savage mirth;
But as you gazed upon its features, they
Changed every instant—to *what*, none could say.

LXXVI

The more intently the ghosts gazed, the less
    Could they distinguish whose the features were;
The Devil himself seemed puzzled even to guess;
    They varied like a dream—now here, now there;
And several people swore from out the press,
    They knew him perfectly; and one could swear
He was his father; upon which another
Was sure he was his mother's cousin's brother:

LXXVII

Another, that he was a duke, or knight,
  An orator, a lawyer, or a priest,
A nabob, a man-midwife; but the wight
  Mysterious changed his countenance at least
As oft as they their minds: though in full sight
  He stood, the puzzle only was increased;
The man was a phantasmagoria in
Himself—he was so volatile and thin.

LXXVIII

The moment that you had pronounced him *one*,
  Presto! his face changed, and he was another;
And when that change was hardly well put on,
  It varied, till I don't think his own mother
(If that he had a mother) would her son
  Have known, he shifted so from one to t'other;
Till guessing from a pleasure grew a task,
At this epistolary 'Iron Mask.'

LXXIX

For sometimes he like Cerberus would seem—
  'Three gentlemen at once' (as sagely says
Good Mrs. Malaprop); then you might deem
  That he was not even *one*; now many rays
Were flashing round him; and now a thick steam
  Hid him from sight—like fogs on London days:
Now Burke, now Tooke, he grew to people's fancies,
And certes often like Sir Philip Francis.

LXXX

I've an hypothesis—'tis quite my own;
  I never let it out till now, for fear
Of doing people harm about the throne,
  And injuring some minister or peer,

[95]

On whom the stigma might perhaps be blown;
   It is—my gentle public, lend thine ear!
'Tis, that what Junius we are wont to call
Was *really, truly*, nobody at all.

LXXXI

I don't see wherefore letters should not be
   Written without hands, since we daily view
Them written without heads; and books, we see,
   Are filled as well without the latter too:
And really till we fix on somebody
   For certain sure to claim them as his due,
Their author, like the Niger's mouth, will bother
The world to say if *there* be mouth or author.

LXXXII

'And who and what art thou?' the Archangel said.
   'For *that* you may consult my title-page,'
Replied this mighty shadow of a shade:
   'If I have kept my secret half an age,
I scarce shall tell it now.'—'Canst thou upbraid,'
   Continued Michael, 'George Rex, or allege
Aught further?' Junius answered, 'You had better
First ask him for *his* answer to my letter:

LXXXIII

'My charges upon record will outlast
   The brass of both his epitaph and tomb.'
'Repent'st thou not,' said Michael, 'of some past
   Exaggeration? something which may doom
Thyself if false, as him if true? Thou wast
   Too bitter—is it not so?—in thy gloom
Of passion?'—'Passion!' cried the phantom dim,
'I loved my country, and I hated him.

[96]

'What I have written, I have written: let
  The rest be on his head or mine!' So spoke
Old 'Nominis Umbra'; and while speaking yet,
  Away he melted in celestial smoke.
Then Satan said to Michael, 'Don't forget
  To call George Washington, and John Horne Tooke,
And Franklin;'—but at this time there was heard
A cry for room, though not a phantom stirred.

At length with jostling, elbowing, and the aid
  Of cherubim appointed to that post,
The devil Asmodeus to the circle made
  His way, and looked as if his journey cost
Some trouble. When his burden down he laid,
  'What's this?' cried Michael; 'why, 'tis not a ghost?'
'I know it,' quoth the incubus; 'but he
Shall be one, if you leave the affair to me.

'Confound the renegado! I have sprained
  My left wing, he's so heavy; one would think
Some of his works about his neck were chained.
  But to the point; while hovering o'er the brink
Of Skiddaw (where as usual it still rained),
  I saw a taper, far below me, wink,
And stooping, caught this fellow at a libel—
No less on history than the Holy Bible.

'The former is the devil's scripture, and
  The latter yours, good Michael: so the affair
Belongs to all of us, you understand.
  I snatched him up just as you see him there,

And brought him off for sentence out of hand:
  I've scarcely been ten minutes in the air—
At least a quarter it can hardly be:
I dare say that his wife is still at tea.'

LXXXVIII

Here Satan said, 'I know this man of old,
  And have expected him for some time here;
A sillier fellow you will scarce behold,
  Or more conceited in his petty sphere:
But surely it was not worth while to fold
  Such trash below your wing, Asmodeus dear:
We had the poor wretch safe (without being bored
With carriage) coming of his own accord.

LXXXIX

'But since he's here, let's see what he has done.'
  'Done!' cried Asmodeus, 'he anticipates
The very business you are now upon,
  And scribbles as if head clerk to the Fates.
Who knows to what his ribaldry may run,
  When such an ass as this, like Balaam's, prates?'
'Let's hear,' quoth Michael, 'what he has to say:
You know we're bound to that in every way.'

XC

Now the bard, glad to get an audience, which
  By no means often was his case below,
Began to cough, and hawk, and hem, and pitch
  His voice into that awful note of woe
To all unhappy hearers within reach
  Of poets when the tide of rhyme's in flow;
But stuck fast with his first hexameter,
Not one of all whose gouty feet would stir.

[98]

But ere the spavined dactyls could be spurred
  Into recitative, in great dismay
Both cherubim and seraphim were heard
  To murmur loudly through their long array;
And Michael rose ere he could get a word
  Of all his foundered verses under way,
And cried, 'For God's sake stop, my friend! 'twere best—
Non Di, non homines—you know the rest.'

A general bustle spread throughout the throng,
  Which seemed to hold all verse in detestation;
The angels had of course enough of song
  When upon service; and the generation
Of ghosts had heard too much in life, not long
  Before, to profit by a new occasion:
The monarch, mute till then, exclaimed, 'What! what!
Pye come again? No more—no more of that!'

The tumult grew; an universal cough
  Convulsed the skies, as during a debate,
When Castlereagh has been up long enough
  (Before he was first minister of state,
I mean—the *slaves hear now*); some cried 'Off, off!'
  As at a farce; till, grown quite desperate,
The bard Saint Peter prayed to interpose
(Himself an author) only for his prose.

The varlet was not an ill-favoured knave;
  A good deal like a vulture in the face,
With a hook nose and a hawk's eye, which gave
  A smart and sharper-looking sort of grace

[99]

To his whole aspect, which, though rather grave,
  Was by no means so ugly as his case;
But that, indeed, was hopeless as can be,
Quite a poetic felony '*de se.*'

XCV

Then Michael blew his trump, and stilled the noise
  With one still greater, as is yet the mode
On earth besides; except some grumbling voice,
  Which now and then will make a slight inroad
Upon decorous silence, few will twice
  Lift up their lungs when fairly overcrowded;
And now the bard could plead his own bad cause,
With all the attitudes of self-applause.

XCVI

He said—(I only give the heads)—he said,
  He meant no harm in scribbling; 'twas his way
Upon all topics; 'twas, besides, his bread,
  Of which he buttered both sides; 'twould delay
Too long the assembly (he was pleased to dread),
  And take up rather more time than a day,
To name his works—he would but cite a few—
'Wat Tyler'—'Rhymes on Blenheim'—'Waterloo.'

XCVII

He had written praises of a regicide;
  He had written praises of all kings whatever;
He had written for republics far and wide,
  And then against them bitterer than ever;
For pantisocracy he once had cried
  Aloud, a scheme less moral than 'twas clever;
Then grew a hearty anti-jacobin—
Had turned his coat—and would have turned his skin.

[100]

He had sung against all battles, and again
　　In their high praise and glory; he had called
Reviewing 'the ungentle craft,' and then
　　Became as base a critic as e'er crawled—
Fed, paid, and pampered by the very men
　　By whom his muse and morals had been mauled:
He had written much blank verse, and blanker prose,
And more of both than any body knows.

XCIX

He had written Wesley's life:—here turning round
　　To Satan, 'Sir, I'm ready to write yours,
In two octavo volumes, nicely bound,
　　With notes and preface, all that most allures
The pious purchaser; and there's no ground
　　For fear, for I can choose my own reviewers:
So let me have the proper documents,
That I may add you to my other saints.'

C

Satan bowed, and was silent. 'Well, if you,
　　With amiable modesty, decline
My offer, what says Michael? There are few
　　Whose memoirs could be rendered more divine.
Mine is a pen of all work; not so new
　　As it was once, but I would make you shine
Like your own trumpet. By the way, my own
Has more of brass in it, and is as well blown.

CI

'But talking about trumpets, here's my Vision!
　　Now you shall judge, all people; yes, you shall
Judge with my judgement, and by my decision
　　Be guided who shall enter heaven or fall.

[101]

I settle all these things by intuition,
    Times present, past, to come, heaven, hell, and all,
Like King Alfonso. When I thus see double,
I save the Deity some worlds of trouble.'

CII

He ceased, and drew forth an MS.; and no
    Persuasion on the part of devils, saints,
Or angels, now could stop the torrent; so
    He read the first three lines of the contents;
But at the fourth, the whole spiritual show
    Had vanished, with variety of scents,
Ambrosial and sulphureous, as they sprang,
Like lightning, off from his 'melodious twang.'

CIII

Those grand heroics acted as a spell;
    The angels stopped their ears and plied their pinions;
The devils ran howling, deafened, down to hell;
    The ghosts fled, gibbering, for their own dominions—
(For 'tis not yet decided where they dwell,
    And I leave every man to his opinions);
Michael took refuge in his trump—but, lo!
His teeth were set on edge, he could not blow!

CIV

Saint Peter, who has hitherto been known
    For an impetuous saint, upraised his keys,
And at the fifth line knocked the poet down;
    Who fell like Phaeton, but more at ease,
Into his lake, for there he did not drown;
    A different web being by the Destinies
Woven for the Laureate's final wreath, whene'er
Reform shall happen either here or there.

He first sank to the bottom—like his works,
  But soon rose to the surface—like himself;
For all corrupted things are buoyed like corks,
  By their own rottenness, light as an elf,
Or wisp that flits o'er a morass: he lurks,
  It may be, still, like dull books on a shelf,
In his own den, to scrawl some 'Life' or 'Vision,'
As Welborn says—'the devil turned precisian.'

As for the rest, to come to the conclusion
  Of this true dream, the telescope is gone
Which kept my optics free from all delusion,
  And showed me what I in my turn have shown;
All I saw farther, in the last confusion,
  Was, that King George slipped into heaven for one;
And when the tumult dwindled to a calm,
I left him practising the hundredth psalm.

from

Don Juan

Canto I, xxxvii–xlviii

A SUPERVISED EDUCATION

XXXVII

Dying intestate, Juan was sole heir
  To a chancery suit, and messuages and lands,
Which, with a long minority and care,
  Promised to turn out well in proper hands:

Inez became sole guardian, which was fair,
    And answered but to nature's just demands;
An only son left with an only mother
Is brought up much more wisely than another.

XXXVIII

Sagest of women, even of widows, she
    Resolved that Juan should be quite a paragon,
And worthy of the noblest pedigree:
    (His sire was of Castile, his dam from Aragon).
Then for accomplishments of chivalry,
    In case our lord the king should go to war again,
He learned the arts of riding, fencing, gunnery,
And how to scale a fortress—or a nunnery.

XXXIX

But that which Donna Inez most desired,
    And saw into herself each day before all
The learned tutors whom for him she hired,
    Was, that his breeding should be strictly moral:
Much into all his studies she inquired,
    And so they were submitted first to her, all,
Arts, sciences, no branch was made a mystery
To Juan's eyes, excepting natural history.

XL

The languages, especially the dead,
    The sciences, and most of all the abstruse,
The arts, at least all such as could be said
    To be the most remote from common use,
In all these he was much and deeply read;
    But not a page of any thing that's loose,
Or hints continuation of the species,
Was ever suffered, lest he should grow vicious.

His classic studies made a little puzzle,
  Because of filthy loves of gods and goddesses,
Who in the earlier ages raised a bustle,
  But never put on pantaloons or bodices;
His reverend tutors had at times a tussle,
  And for their Æneids, Iliads, and Odysseys,
Were forced to make an odd sort of apology,
For Donna Inez dreaded the Mythology.

XLII

Ovid's a rake, as half his verses show him,
  Anacreon's morals are a still worse sample,
Catullus scarcely has a decent poem,
  I don't think Sappho's Ode a good example,
Although Longinus tells us there is no hymn
  Where the sublime soars forth on wings more ample;
But Virgil's songs are pure, except that horrid one
Beginning with 'Formosum Pastor Corydon.'

XLIII

Lucretius' irreligion is too strong
  For early stomachs, to prove wholesome food;
I can't help thinking Juvenal was wrong,
  Although no doubt his real intent was good,
For speaking out so plainly in his song,
  So much indeed as to be downright rude;
And then what proper person can be partial
To all those nauseous epigrams of Martial?

XLIV

Juan was taught from out the best edition,
  Expurgated by learned men, who place,
Judiciously, from out the schoolboy's vision,
  The grosser parts; but, fearful to deface

[105]

Too much their modest bard by this omission,
  And pitying sore this mutilated case,
They only add them all in an appendix,
Which saves, in fact, the trouble of an index.

XLV

For there we have them all 'at one fell swoop,'
  Instead of being scattered through the pages;
They stand forth marshalled in a handsome troop,
  To meet the ingenuous youth of future ages,
Till some less rigid editor shall stoop
  To call them back into their separate cages,
Instead of standing staring all together,
Like garden gods—and not so decent either.

XLVI

The Missal too (it was the family Missal)
  Was ornamented in a sort of way
Which ancient mass-books often are, and this all
  Kinds of grotesques illumined; and how they,
Who saw those figures on the margin kiss all,
  Could turn their optics to the text and pray,
Is more than I know—But Don Juan's mother
Kept this herself, and gave her son another.

XLVII

Sermons he read, and lectures he endured,
  And homilies, and lives of all the saints;
To Jerome and to Chrysostom inured,
  He did not take such studies for restraints;
But how faith is acquired, and then ensured,
  So well not one of the aforesaid paints
As Saint Augustine in his fine Confessions,
Which make the reader envy his transgressions.

XLVIII

This, too, was a sealed book to little Juan—
  I can't but say that his mamma was right,
If such an education was the true one.
  She scarcely trusted him from out her sight;
Her maids were old, and if she took a new one,
  You might be sure she was a perfect fright,
She did this during even her husband's life—
I recommend as much to every wife.

Canto I, lx–lxxxv

MEDITERRANEAN TEMPTATION

LX

Her eye (I'm very fond of handsome eyes)
  Was large and dark, suppressing half its fire
Until she spoke, then through its soft disguise
  Flashed an expression more of pride than ire,
And love than either; and there would arise
  A something in them which was not desire,
But would have been, perhaps, but for the soul
Which struggled through and chastened down the whole.

LXI

Her glossy hair was clustered o'er a brow
  Bright with intelligence, and fair, and smooth;
Her eyebrow's shape was like the aërial bow,
  Her cheek all purple with the beam of youth,
Mounting, at times, to a transparent glow,
  As if her veins ran lightning; she, in sooth,
Possessed an air and grace by no means common:
Her stature tall—I hate a dumpy woman.

Wedded she was some years, and to a man
  Of fifty, and such husbands are in plenty;
And yet, I think, instead of such a ONE
  'Twere better to have TWO of five-and-twenty,
Especially in countries near the sun:
  And now I think on't, 'mi vien in mente,'
Ladies even of the most uneasy virtue
Prefer a spouse whose age is short of thirty.

'Tis a sad thing, I cannot choose but say,
  And all the fault of that indecent sun,
Who cannot leave alone our helpless clay,
  But will keep baking, broiling, burning on,
That howsoever people fast and pray,
  The flesh is frail, and so the soul undone:
What men call gallantry, and gods adultery,
Is much more common where the climate's sultry.

Happy the nations of the moral North!
  Where all is virtue, and the winter season
Sends sin, without a rag on, shivering forth
  ('Twas snow that brought St. Anthony to reason);
Where juries cast up what a wife is worth,
  By laying whate'er sum, in mulct, they please on
The lover, who must pay a handsome price,
Because it is a marketable vice.

Alfonso was the name of Julia's lord,
  A man well looking for his years, and who
Was neither much beloved nor yet abhorred:
  They lived together as most people do,

Suffering each other's foibles by accord,
    And not exactly either *one* or *two*;
Yet he was jealous, though he did not show it,
For jealousy dislikes the world to know it.

LXVI

Julia was—yet I never could see why—
    With Donna Inez quite a favourite friend;
Between their tastes there was small sympathy,
    For not a line had Julia ever penned:
Some people whisper (but, no doubt, they lie,
    For malice still imputes some private end)
That Inez had, ere Don Alfonso's marriage,
Forgot with him her very prudent carriage;

LXVII

And that still keeping up the old connection,
    Which time had lately rendered much more chaste,
She took his lady also in affection,
    And certainly this course was much the best:
She flattered Julia with her sage protection,
    And complimented Don Alfonso's taste;
And if she could not (who can?) silence scandal,
At least she left it a more slender handle.

LXVIII

I can't tell whether Julia saw the affair
    With other people's eyes, or if her own
Discoveries made, but none could be aware
    Of this, at least no symptom e'er was shown;
Perhaps she did not know, or did not care,
    Indifferent from the first, or callous grown:
I'm really puzzled what to think or say,
She kept her counsel in so close a way.

[109]

Juan she saw, and, as a pretty child,
  Caressed him often—such a thing might be
Quite innocently done, and harmless styled,
  When she had twenty years, and thirteen he;
But I am not so sure I should have smiled
  When he was sixteen, Julia twenty-three;
These few short years make wondrous alterations,
Particularly amongst sun-burnt nations.

Whate'er the cause might be, they had become
  Changed; for the dame grew distant, the youth shy,
Their looks cast down, their greetings almost dumb,
  And much embarrassment in either eye;
There surely will be little doubt with some
  That Donna Julia knew the reason why,
But as for Juan, he had no more notion
Than he who never saw the sea of ocean.

Yet Julia's very coldness still was kind,
  And tremulously gentle her small hand
Withdrew itself from his, but left behind
  A little pressure, thrilling, and so bland
And slight, so very slight, that to the mind
  'Twas but a doubt; but ne'er magician's wand
Wrought change with all Armida's fairy art
Like what this light touch left on Juan's heart.

And if she met him, though she smiled no more,
  She looked a sadness sweeter than her smile,
As if her heart had deeper thoughts in store
  She must not own, but cherished more the while

For that compression in its burning core;
   Even innocence itself has many a wile,
And will not dare to trust itself with truth,
And love is taught hypocrisy from youth.

LXXIII

But passion most dissembles, yet betrays
   Even by its darkness; as the blackest sky
Foretells the heaviest tempest, it displays
   Its workings through the vainly guarded eye,
And in whatever aspect it arrays
   Itself, 'tis still the same hypocrisy;
Coldness or anger, even disdain or hate,
Are masks it often wears, and still too late.

LXXIV

Then there were sighs, the deeper for suppression,
   And stolen glances sweeter for the theft,
And burning blushes, though for no transgression,
   Tremblings when met, and restlessness when left;
All these are little preludes to possession,
   Of which young passion cannot be bereft,
And merely tend to show how greatly love is
Embarrassed at first starting with a novice.

LXXV

Poor Julia's heart was in an awkward state;
   She felt it going, and resolved to make
The noblest efforts for herself and mate,
   For honour's, pride's, religion's, virtue's sake:
Her resolutions were most truly great,
   And almost might have made a Tarquin quake:
She prayed the Virgin Mary for her grace,
As being the best judge of a lady's case.

[111]

LXXVI

She vowed she never would see Juan more,
   And next day paid a visit to his mother,
And looked extremely at the opening door,
   Which, by the Virgin's grace, let in another;
Grateful she was, and yet a little sore—
   Again it opens, it can be no other,
'Tis surely Juan now—No! I'm afraid
That night the Virgin was no further prayed.

LXXVII

She now determined that a virtuous woman
   Should rather face and overcome temptation,
That flight was base and dastardly, and no man
   Should ever give her heart the least sensation;
That is to say, a thought beyond the common
   Preference, that we must feel upon occasion,
For people who are pleasanter than others,
But then they only seem so many brothers.

LXXVIII

And even if by chance—and who can tell?
   The devil's so very sly—she could discover
That all within was not so very well,
   And, if still free, that such or such a lover
Might please perhaps, a virtuous wife can quell
   Such thoughts, and be the better when they're over;
And if the man should ask, 'tis but denial:
I recommend young ladies to make trial.

LXXIX

And then there are such things as love divine,
   Bright and immaculate, unmixed and pure,
Such as the angels think so very fine,
   And matrons, who would be no less secure,

Platonic, perfect, 'just such love as mine:'
   Thus Julia said—and thought so, to be sure:
And so I'd have her think, were I the man
On whom her reveries celestial ran.

LXXX

Such love is innocent, and may exist
   Between young persons without any danger:
A hand may first, and then a lip be kist;
   For my part, to such doings I'm a stranger,
But *hear* these freedoms form the utmost list
   Of all o'er which such love may be a ranger:
If people go beyond, 'tis quite a crime,
But not my fault—I tell them all in time.

LXXXI

Love, then, but love within its proper limits,
   Was Julia's innocent determination
In young Don Juan's favour, and to him its
   Exertion might be useful on occasion;
And, lighted at too pure a shrine to dim its
   Ethereal lustre, with what sweet persuasion,
He might be taught, by love and her together—
I really don't know what, nor Julia either.

LXXXII

Fraught with this fine intention, and well fenced
   In mail of proof—her purity of soul,
She, for the future of her strength convinced,
   And that her honour was a rock, or mole,
Exceeding sagely from that hour dispensed
   With any kind of troublesome control;
But whether Julia to the task was equal
Is that which must be mentioned in the sequel.

[113]

LXXXIII

Her plan she deemed both innocent and feasible,
    And, surely, with a stripling of sixteen
Not scandal's fangs could seize on much that's seizable,
    Or if they did so, satisfied to mean
Nothing but what was good, her breast was peaceable:
    A quiet conscience makes one so serene!
Christians have burnt each other, quite persuaded
That all the Apostles would have done as they did.

LXXXIV

And if in the mean time her husband died,
    But Heaven forbid that such a thought should cross
Her brain, though in a dream! (and then she sighed)
    Never could she survive that common loss;
But just suppose that moment should betide,
    I only say suppose it—*inter nos*.
(This should be *entre nous*, for Julia thought
In French, but then the rhyme would go for nought.)

LXXXV

I only say, suppose this supposition:
    Juan being then grown up to man's estate
Would fully suit a widow of condition,
    Even seven years hence it would not be too late;
And in the interim (to pursue this vision)
    The mischief, after all, could not be great,
For he would learn the rudiments of love,
I mean the seraph way of those above.

THE SEQUEL

CLXIX

What's to be done? Alfonso will be back
  The moment he has sent his fools away.
Antonia's skill was put upon the rack,
  But no device could be brought into play—
And how to parry the renewed attack?
  Besides, it wanted but few hours of day:
Antonia puzzled; Julia did not speak,
But pressed her bloodless lip to Juan's cheek.

CLXX

He turned his lip to hers, and with his hand
  Called back the tangles of her wandering hair;
Even then their love they could not all command,
  And half forgot their danger and despair:
Antonia's patience now was at a stand—
  'Come, come, 'tis no time now for fooling there,'
She whispered, in great wrath—'I must deposit
This pretty gentleman within the closet:

CLXXI

'Pray, keep your nonsense for some luckier night—
  Who can have put my master in this mood?
What will become on't—I'm in such a fright,
  The Devil's in the urchin, and no good—
Is this a time for giggling? this a plight?
  Why, don't you know that it may end in blood?
You'll lose your life, and I shall lose my place,
My mistress all, for that half-girlish face.

'Had it but been for a stout cavalier
  Of twenty-five or thirty—(come, make haste)
But for a child, what piece of work is here!
  I really, madam, wonder at your taste—
(Come, sir, get in)—my master must be near:
  There, for the present, at the least, he's fast,
And if we can but till the morning keep
Our counsel—(Juan, mind, you must not sleep).'

Now, Don Alfonso entering, but alone,
  Closed the oration of the trusty maid:
She loitered, and he told her to be gone,
  An order somewhat sullenly obeyed;
However, present remedy was none,
  And no great good seemed answered if she stayed;
Regarding both with slow and sidelong view,
She snuffed the candle, curtsied, and withdrew.

Alfonso paused a minute—then begun
  Some strange excuses for his late proceedings;
He would not justify what he had done,
  To say the best, it was extreme ill-breeding;
But there were ample reasons for it, none
  Of which he specified in this his pleading:
His speech was a fine sample, on the whole,
Of rhetoric, which the learned call 'rigmarole.'

Julia said nought; though all the while there rose
  A ready answer, which at once enables
A matron, who her husband's foible knows,
  By a few timely words to turn the tables,

[116]

Which, if it does not silence, still must pose,—
  Even if it should comprise a pack of fables;
'Tis to retort with firmness, and when he
Suspects with *one*, do you reproach with *three*.

CLXXVI

Julia, in fact, had tolerable grounds,—
  Alfonso's loves with Inez were well known;
But whether 'twas that one's own guilt confounds—
  But that can't be, as has been often shown,
A lady with apologies abounds;—
  It might be that her silence sprang alone
From delicacy to Don Juan's ear,
To whom she knew his mother's fame was dear.

CLXXVII

There might be one more motive, which makes two,
  Alfonso ne'er to Juan had alluded,—
Mentioned his jealousy, but never who
  Had been the happy lover, he concluded,
Concealed amongst his premises; 'tis true,
  His mind the more o'er this its mystery brooded;
To speak of Inez now were, one may say,
Like throwing Juan in Alfonso's way.

CLXXVIII

A hint, in tender cases, is enough;
  Silence is best, besides there is a *tact*—
(That modern phrase appears to me sad stuff,
  But it will serve to keep my verse compact)—
Which keeps, when pushed by questions rather rough,
  A lady always distant from the fact:
The charming creatures lie with such a grace,
There's nothing so becoming to the face.

[117]

CLXXIX

They blush, and we believe them; at least I
  Have always done so; 'tis of no great use,
In any case, attempting a reply,
  For then their eloquence grows quite profuse;
And when at length they're out of breath, they sigh,
  And cast their languid eyes down, and let loose
A tear or two, and then we make it up;
And then—and then—and then—sit down and sup.

CLXXX

Alfonso closed his speech, and begged her pardon,
  Which Julia half withheld, and then half granted,
And laid conditions, he thought very hard, on,
  Denying several little things he wanted:
He stood like Adam lingering near his garden,
  With useless penitence perplexed and haunted,
Beseeching she no further would refuse,
When, lo! he stumbled o'er a pair of shoes.

CLXXXI

A pair of shoes!—what then? not much, if they
  Are such as fit with ladies' feet, but these
(No one can tell how much I grieve to say)
  Were masculine; to see them, and to seize,
Was but a moment's act.—Ah! well-a-day!
  My teeth begin to chatter, my veins freeze—
Alfonso first examined well their fashion,
And then flew out into another passion.

CLXXXII

He left the room for his relinquished sword,
  And Julia instant to the closet flew.
'Fly, Juan, fly! for heaven's sake—not a word—
  The door is open—you may yet slip through

[118]

The passage you so often have explored—
   Here is the garden-key—Fly—fly—Adieu!
Haste—haste! I hear Alfonso's hurrying feet—
Day has not broke—there's no one in the street.'

CLXXXIII

None can say that this was not good advice,
   The only mischief was, it came too late;
Of all experience 'tis the usual price,
   A sort of income-tax laid on by fate:
Juan had reached the room-door in a trice,
   And might have done so by the garden-gate,
But met Alfonso in his dressing-gown,
Who threatened death—so Juan knocked him down.

CLXXXIV

Dire was the scuffle, and out went the light;
   Antonia cried out 'Rape!' and Julia 'Fire!'
But not a servant stirred to aid the fight.
   Alfonso, pommelled to his heart's desire,
Swore lustily he'd be revenged this night;
   And Juan, too, blasphemed an octave higher;
His blood was up: though young, he was a Tartar,
And not at all disposed to prove a martyr.

CLXXXV

Alfonso's sword had dropped ere he could draw it,
   And they continued battling hand to hand,
For Juan very luckily ne'er saw it;
   His temper not being under great command,
If at that moment he had chanced to claw it,
   Alfonso's days had not been in the land
Much longer.—Think of husbands', lovers' lives!
And how ye may be doubly widows—wives!

[119]

Alfonso grappled to detain the foe,
　And Juan throttled him to get away,
And blood ('twas from the nose) began to flow;
　At last, as they more faintly wrestling lay,
Juan contrived to give an awkward blow,
　And then his only garment quite gave way;
He fled, like Joseph, leaving it; but there,
I doubt, all likeness ends between the pair.

Lights came at length, and men, and maids, who found
　An awkward spectacle their eyes before;
Antonia in hysterics, Julia swooned,
　Alfonso leaning, breathless, by the door;
Some half-torn drapery scattered on the ground,
　Some blood, and several footsteps, but no more:
Juan the gate gained, turned the key about,
And liking not the inside, locked the out.

Here ends this canto.—Need I sing, or say,
　How Juan, naked, favoured by the night,
Who favours what she should not, found his way,
　And reached his home in an unseemly plight?
The pleasant scandal which arose next day,
　The nine day's wonder which was brought to light,
And how Alfonso sued for a divorce,
Were in the English newspapers, of course.

If you would like to see the whole proceedings,
　The depositions and the cause at full,
The names of all the witnesses, the pleadings
　Of counsel to nonsuit, or to annul,

[120]

There's more than one edition, and the readings
　　Are various, but they none of them are dull;
The best is that in short-hand ta'en by Gurney,
Who to Madrid on purpose made a journey.

CXC

But Donna Inez, to divert the train
　　Of one of the most circulating scandals
That had for centuries been known in Spain,
　　At least since the retirement of the Vandals,
First vowed (and never had she vowed in vain)
　　To Virgin Mary several pounds of candles;
And then, by the advice of some old ladies,
She sent her son to be shipped off from Cadiz.

CXCI

She had resolved that he should travel through
　　All European climes, by land or sea,
To mend his former morals, and get new,
　　Especially in France and Italy,
(At least this is the thing most people do.)
　　Julia was sent into a convent: she
Grieved, but, perhaps, her feelings may be better
Shown in the following copy of her Letter:—

CXCII

'They tell me 'tis decided you depart:
　　'Tis wise—'tis well, but not the less a pain;
I have no further claim on your young heart,
　　Mine is the victim, and would be again:
To love too much has been the only art
　　I used;—I write in haste, and if a stain
Be on this sheet, 'tis not what it appears;
My eyeballs burn and throb, but have no tears.

[121]

'I loved, I love you, for this love have lost
  State, station, heaven, mankind's, my own esteem,
And yet cannot regret what it hath cost,
  So dear is still the memory of that dream;
Yet, if I name my guilt, 'tis not to boast,
  None can deem harshlier of me than I deem:
I trace this scrawl because I cannot rest—
I've nothing to reproach or to request.

CXCIV

'Man's love is of man's life a thing apart,
  'Tis woman's whole existence; man may range
The court, camp, church, the vessel, and the mart,
  Sword, gown, gain, glory, offer in exchange
Pride, fame, ambition, to fill up his heart,
  And few there are whom these cannot estrange;
Men have all these resources, we but one,
To love again, and be again undone.'

Canto III, lxxviii–c

THE ISLES OF GREECE

A Noble Hymn in the Context of Poetical Lies

LXXVIII

And now they were diverted by their suite,
  Dwarfs, dancing-girls, black eunuchs, and a poet,
Which made their new establishment complete;
  The last was of great fame, and liked to show it
His verses rarely wanted their due feet—

[122]

And for his theme—he seldom sung below it,
He being paid to satirise or flatter,
As the psalm says, 'inditing a good matter.'

He praised the present, and abused the past,
    Reversing the good custom of old days,
An Eastern anti-jacobin at last
    He turned, preferring pudding to *no* praise—
For some few years his lot had been o'ercast
    By his seeming independent in his lays,
But now he sung the Sultan and the Pacha
With truth like Southey, and with verse like Crashaw.

He was a man who had seen many changes,
    And always changed as true as any needle;
His polar star being one which rather ranges,
    And not the fixed—he knew the way to wheedle:
So vile he 'scaped the doom which oft avenges;
    And being fluent (save indeed when fee'd ill),
He lied with such a fervour of intention—
There was no doubt he earned his laureate pension.

But he had genius,—when a turncoat has it,
    The 'Vates irritabilis' takes care
That without notice few full moons shall pass it;
    Even good men like to make the public stare:—
But to my subject—let me see—what was it?—
    Oh!—the third canto—and the pretty pair—
Their loves, and feasts, and house, and dress, and mode
Of living in their insular abode.

LXXXII

Their poet, a sad trimmer, but no less
　In company a very pleasant fellow,
Had been the favourite of full many a mess
　Of men, and made them speeches when half mellow;
And though his meaning they could rarely guess,
　Yet still they deigned to hiccup or to bellow
The glorious meed of popular applause,
Of which the first ne'er knows the second cause.

LXXXIII

But now being lifted into high society,
　And having picked up several odds and ends
Of free thoughts in his travels, for variety,
　He deemed, being in a lone isle, among friends,
That without any danger of a riot, he
　Might for long lying make himself amends;
And singing as he sung in his warm youth,
Agree to a short armistice with truth.

LXXXIV

He had travelled 'mongst the Arabs, Turks, and Franks,
　And knew the self-loves of the different nations;
And having lived with people of all ranks,
　Had something ready upon most occasions—
Which got him a few presents and some thanks.
　He varied with some skill his adulations;
To 'do at Rome as Romans do,' a piece
Of conduct was which he observed in Greece.

LXXXV

Thus, usually, when he was asked to sing,
　He gave the different nations something national;
'Twas all the same to him—'God save the king,'
　Or 'Ça ira,' according to the fashion all:

His muse made increment of any thing,
　　From the high lyric down to the low rational:
If Pindar sang horse-races, what should hinder
Himself from being as pliable as Pindar?

LXXXVI

In France for instance, he would write a chanson;
　　In England a six canto quarto tale;
In Spain he'd make a ballad or romance on
　　The last war—much the same in Portugal;
In Germany, the Pegasus he'd prance on
　　Would be old Goethe's—(see what says de Staël);
In Italy he'd ape the 'Trecentisti;'
In Greece, he'd sing some sort of hymn like this t' ye:

1

　　The isles of Greece, the isle of Greece!
　　　　Where burning Sappho loved and sung,
　　Where grew the arts of war and peace,
　　　　Where Delos rose, and Phœbus sprung!
　　Eternal summer gilds them yet,
　　But all, except their sun, is set.

2

　　The Scian and the Teian muse,
　　　　The hero's harp, the lover's lute,
　　Have found the fame your shores refuse;
　　　　Their place of birth alone is mute
　　To sounds which echo further west
　　Than your sires' 'Islands of the Blest.'

3

　　The mountains look on Marathon—
　　　　And Marathon looks on the sea;
　　And musing there an hour alone,

I dreamed that Greece might still be free;
For standing on the Persians' grave,
I could not deem myself a slave.

4

A king sate on the rocky brow
    Which looks o'er sea-born Salamis;
And ships, by thousands, lay below,
    And men in nations;—all were his!
He counted them at break of day—
And when the sun set where were they?

5

And where are they? and where art thou,
    My country? On thy voiceless shore
The heroic lay is tuneless now—
    The heroic bosom beats no more!
And must thy lyre, so long divine,
Degenerate into hands like mine?

6

'Tis something, in the dearth of fame,
    Though linked among a fettered race,
To feel at least a patriot's shame,
    Even as I sing, suffuse my face;
For what is left the poet here?
For Greeks a blush—for Greece a tear.

7

Must *we* but weep o'er days more blest?
    Must *we* but blush?—Our fathers bled.
Earth! render back from out thy breast
    A remnant of our Spartan dead!
Of the three hundred grant but three,
To make a new Thermopylae!

What, silent still? and silent all?
  Ah! no;—the voices of the dead
Sound like a distant torrent's fall,
  And answer, 'Let one living head,
But one arise,—we come, we come!'
'Tis but the living who are dumb.

In vain—in vain: strike other chords;
  Fill high the cup with Samian wine!
Leave battles to the Turkish hordes,
  And shed the blood of Scio's vine!
Hark! rising to the ignoble call—
How answers each bold Bacchanal!

You have the Pyrrhic dance as yet;
  Where is the Pyrrhic phalanx gone?
Of two such lessons, why forget
  The nobler and the manlier one?
You have the letters Cadmus gave—
Think ye he meant them for a slave?

Fill high the bowl with Samian wine!
  We will not think of themes like these!
It made Anacreon's song divine:
  He served—but served Polycrates—
A tyrant; but our masters then
Were still, at least, our countrymen.

The tyrant of the Chersonese
  Was freedom's best and bravest friend;
That tyrant was Miltiades!

Oh! that the present hour would lend
Another despot of the kind!
Such chains as his were sure to bind.

13

Fill high the bowl with Samian wine!
   On Suli's rock, and Parga's shore,
Exists the remnant of a line
   Such as the Doric mothers bore;
And there, perhaps, some seed is sown.
There Heracleidan blood might own.

14

Trust not for freedom to the Franks—
   They have a king who buys and sells:
In native swords, and native ranks,
   The only hope of courage dwells:
But Turkish force, and Latin fraud,
Would break your shield, however broad.

15

Fill high the bowl with Samian wine!
   Our virgins dance beneath the shade—
I see their glorious black eyes shine;
   But gazing on each glowing maid,
My own the burning tear-drop laves,
To think such breasts must suckle slaves.

16

Place me on Sunium's marbled steep,
   Where nothing, save the waves and I,
May hear our mutual murmurs sweep;
   There, swan-like, let me sing and die:
A land of slaves shall ne'er be mine—
Dash down yon cup of Samian wine!

Thus sung, or would, or could, or should have sung,
  The modern Greek, in tolerable verse;
If not like Orpheus quite, when Greece was young,
  Yet in these times he might have done much worse:
His strain displayed some feeling—right or wrong;
  And feeling, in a poet, is the source
Of others' feeling; but they are such liars,
And take all colours—like the hands of dyers.

But words are things, and a small drop of ink,
  Falling like dew, upon a thought, produces
That which makes thousands, perhaps millions, think;
  'Tis strange, the shortest letter which man uses
Instead of speech, may form a lasting link
  Of ages; to what straits old Time reduces
Frail man, when paper—even a rag like this,
Survives himself, his tomb, and all that's his.

And when his bones are dust, his grave a blank,
  His station, generation, even his nation,
Become a thing, or nothing, save to rank
  In chronological commemoration,
Some dull MS. oblivion long has sank,
  Or graven stone found in a barrack's station
In digging the foundation of a closet,
May turn his name up, as a rare deposit.

And glory long has made the sages smile;
  'Tis something, nothing, words, illusion, wind—
Depending more upon the historian's style
  Than on the name a person leaves behind:

Troy owes to Homer what whist owes to Hoyle:
　　The present century was growing blind
To the great Marlborough's skill in giving knocks,
Until his late Life by Archdeacon Coxe.

XCI

Milton's the prince of poets—so we say;
　　A little heavy, but no less divine:
An independent being in his day—
　　Learnèd, pious, temperate in love and wine;
But his life falling into Johnson's way,
　　We're told this great high priest of all the Nine
Was whipt at college—a harsh sire—odd spouse,
For the first Mrs. Milton left his house.

XCII

All these are, *certes*, entertaining facts,
　　Like Shakspeare's stealing deer, Lord Bacon's brides;
Like Titus' youth, and Cæsar's earliest acts;
　　Like Burns (whom Doctor Currie well describes);
Like Cromwell's pranks;—but although truth exacts
　　These amiable descriptions from the scribes,
As most essential to their hero's story,
They do not much contribute to his glory.

XCIII

All are not moralists, like Southey, when
　　He prated to the world of 'Pantisocrasy;'
Or Wordsworth unexcised, unhired, who then
　　Seasoned his pedlar poems with democracy;
Or Coleridge, long before his flighty pen
　　Let to the Morning Post its aristocracy;
When he and Southey, following the same path,
Espoused two partners (milliners of Bath).

[130]

Such names at present cut a convict figure,
    The very Botany Bay in moral geography;
Their loyal treason, renegado rigour,
    Are good manure for their more bare biography,
Wordsworth's last quarto, by the way, is bigger
    Than any since the birthday of typography;
A drowzy frowzy poem, called the 'Excursion,'
Writ in a manner which is my aversion.

He there builds up a formidable dyke
    Between his own and others' intellect;
But Wordsworth's poem, and his followers, like
    Joanna Southcote's Shiloh, and her sect,
Are things which in this century don't strike
    The public mind,—so few are the elect;
And the new births of both their stale virginities
Have proved but dropsies, taken for divinities.

But let me to my story: I must own,
    If I have any fault, it is digression,
Leaving my people to proceed alone,
    While I soliloquize beyond expression:
But these are my addresses from the throne,
    Which put off business to the ensuing session:
Forgetting each omission is a loss to
The world, not quite so great as Ariosto.

I know that what our neighbours call '*longueurs*,'
    (We've not so good a *word*, but have the *thing*,
In that complete perfection which ensures

An epic from Bob Southey every Spring—)
Form not the true temptation which allures
   The reader; but 'twould not be hard to bring
Some fine examples of the *épopée*,
To prove its grand ingredient is *ennui*.

XCVIII

We learn from Horace, 'Homer sometimes sleeps;'
   We feel without him, Wordsworth sometimes wakes,—
To show with what complacency he creeps,
   With his dear '*Waggoners*,' around his lakes.
He wishes for 'a boat' to sail the deeps—
   Of ocean?—No, of air; and then he makes
Another outcry for 'a little boat,'
And drivels seas to set it well afloat.'

XCIX

If he must fain sweep o'er the ethereal plain,
   And Pegasus runs restive in his 'Waggon,'
Could he not beg the loan of Charles's Wain?
   Or pray Medea for a single dragon?
Or if, too classic for his vulgar brain,
   He feared his neck to venture such a nag on,
And he must needs mount nearer to the moon,
Could not the blockhead ask for a balloon?

C

'Pedlars,' and 'Boats,' and 'Waggons!' Oh! ye shades
   Of Pope and Dryden, are we come to this?
That trash of such sort not alone evades
   Contempt, but from the bathos' vast abyss
Floats scumlike uppermost, and these Jack Cades
   Of sense and song above your graves may hiss—
The 'little boatman' and his 'Peter Bell'
Can sneer at him who drew 'Achitophel!'

INTENSITIES OF BLUE

CVIII

Oh! ye, who make the fortunes of all books!
  Benign Ceruleans of the second sex!
Who advertise new poems by your looks,
  Your 'imprimatur' will ye not annex?
What! must I go to the oblivious cooks,
  Those Cornish plunderers of Parnassian wrecks?
Ah! must I then the only minstrel be,
Proscribed from tasting your Castalian tea?

CIX

What! can I prove 'a lion' then no more?
  A ball-room bard, a foolscap, hot-press darling?
To bear the compliments of many a bore,
  And sigh, 'I can't get out,' like Yorick's starling;
Why then I'll swear, as poet Wordy swore,
  (Because the world won't read him, always snarling)
That taste is gone, that fame is but a lottery,
Drawn by the blue-coat misses of a coterie.

CX

Oh! 'darkly, deeply, beautifully blue,'
  As some one somewhere sings about the sky,
And I, ye learned ladies, say of you;
  They say your stockings are so—(Heaven knows why,
I have examined few pair of that hue);
  Blue as the garters which serenely lie
Round the Patrician left-legs, which adorn
The festal midnight, and the levée morn.

CXI

Yet some of you are most seraphic creatures—
   But times are altered since, a rhyming lover,
You read my stanzas, and I read your features:
   And—but no matter, all those things are over;
Still I have no dislike to learnèd natures,
   For sometimes such a world of virtues cover;
I knew one woman of that purple school,
The loveliest, chastest, best, but—quite a fool.

CXII

Humboldt, 'the first of travellers,' but not
   The last, if late accounts be accurate,
Invented, by some name I have forgot,
   As well as the sublime discovery's date,
An airy instrument, with which he sought
   To ascertain the atmospheric state,
By measuring 'the *intensity of blue:*'
Oh, Lady Daphne! let me measure you!

Canto VI, xxi–lxxxv

A TURKISH FARCE

XXI

A scolding wife, a sullen son, a bill
   To pay, unpaid, protested or discounted
At a per-centage; a child cross, dog ill,
   A favourite horse fallen lame just as he's mounted,
A bad old woman making a worse will,
   Which leaves you minus of the cash you counted
As certain;—these are paltry things, and yet
I've rarely seen the man they did not fret.

XXII

I'm a philosopher; confound them all!
   Bills, beasts, and men, and—no! *not* womankind!
With one good hearty curse I vent my gall,
   And then my stoicism leaves nought behind
Which it can either pain or evil call,
   And I can give my whole soul up to mind;
Though what *is* soul, or mind, their birth or growth,
Is more than I know—the deuce take them both!

So now all things are damned one feels at ease,
   As after reading Athanasius' curse,
Which doth your true believer so much please:
   I doubt if any now could make it worse
O'er his worst enemy when at his knees,
   'Tis so sententious, positive, and terse,
And decorates the Book of Common Prayer,
As doth a rainbow the just clearing air.

XXIV

Gulbeyaz and her lord were sleeping, or
   At least one of them!—Oh, the heavy night,
When wicked wives, who love some bachelor,
   Lie down in dudgeon to sigh for the light
Of the grey morning, and look vainly for
   Its twinkle through the lattice dusky quite—
To toss, to tumble, doze, revive, and quake
Lest their too lawful bed-fellow should wake!

These are beneath the canopy of heaven,
   Also beneath the canopy of beds
Four-posted and silk-curtained, which are given
   For rich men and their brides to lay their heads

Upon, in sheets white as what bards call 'driven
  Snow.' Well! 'tis all hap-hazard when one weds.
Gulbeyaz was an empress, but had been
Perhaps as wretched if a *peasant's quean*.

XXVI

Don Juan in his feminine disguise,
  With all the damsels in their long array,
Had bowed themselves before the imperial eyes,
  And at the usual signal ta'en their way
Back to their chambers, those long galleries
  In the seraglio, where the ladies lay
Their delicate limbs; a thousand bosoms there
Beating for love, as the caged bird's for air.

XXVII

I love the sex, and sometimes would reverse
  The tyrant's wish, 'that mankind only had
One neck, which he with one fell stroke might pierce:'
  My wish is quite as wide, but not so bad,
And much more tender on the whole than fierce;
  It being (not *now*, but only while a lad)
That womankind had but one rosy mouth,
To kiss them all at once from North to South.

XXVIII

Oh, enviable Briareus! with thy hands
  And heads, if thou hast all things multiplied
In such proportion!—But my Muse withstands
  The giant thought of being a Titan's bride,
Or travelling in Patagonian lands;
  So let us back to Lilliput, and guide
Our hero through the labyrinth of love
In which we left him several lines above.

XXIX

He went forth with the lovely Odalisques,
　At the given signal joined to their array;
And though he certainly ran many risks,
　Yet he could not at times keep, by the way,
(Although the consequences of such frisks
　Are worse than the worst damages men pay
In moral England, where the thing's a tax,)
From ogling all their charms from breasts to backs.

XXX

Still he forgot not his disguise:—along
　The galleries from room to room they walked,
A virgin-like and edifying throng,
　By eunuchs flanked; while at their head there stalked
A dame who kept up discipline among
　The female ranks, so that none stirred or talked,
Without her sanction on their she-parades:
Her title was 'the Mother of the Maids.'

XXXI

Whether she was 'a mother,' I know not,
　Or whether they were maids who called her mother;
But this is her seraglio title, got
　I know not how, but good as any other;
So Cantemir can tell you, or De Tott:
　Her office was to keep aloof or smother
All bad propensities in fifteen hundred
Young women, and correct them when they blundered.

XXXII

A goodly sinecure, no doubt! but made
　More easy by the absence of all men—
Except His Majesty,—who, with her aid,
　And guards, and bolts, and walls, and now and then,

A slight example, just to cast a shade
　　Along the rest, contrived to keep this den
Of beauties cool as an Italian convent,
Where all the passions have, alas! but one vent.

XXXIII

And what is that? Devotion, doubtless—how
　　Could you ask such a question?—but we will
Continue. As I said, this goodly row
　　Of ladies of all countries at the will
Of one good man, with stately march and slow,
　　Like water-lilies floating down a rill—
Or rather lake—for *rills* do not run *slowly,*—
Paced on most maiden-like and melancholy.

XXXIV

But when they reached their own apartments, there,
　　Like birds, or boys, or bedlamites broke loose,
Waves at spring-tide, or women anywhere
　　When freed from bonds (which are of no great use
After all), or like Irish at a fair,
　　Their guards being gone, and as it were a truce
Established between them and bondage, they
Began to sing, dance, chatter, smile, and play.

XXXV

Their talk, of course, ran most on the newcomer;
　　Her shape, her hair, her air, her everything:
Some thought her dress did not so much become her,
　　Or wondered at her ears without a ring;
Some said her years were getting nigh their summer,
　　Others contended they were but in spring;
Some thought her rather masculine in height,
While others wished that she had been so quite.

[138]

XXXVI

But no one doubted on the whole, that she
  Was what her dress bespoke, a damsel fair,
And fresh, and 'beautiful exceedingly,'
  Who with the brightest Georgians might compare:
They wondered how Gulbeyaz, too, could be
  So silly as to buy slaves who might share
(If that his Highness wearied of his bride)
Her throne and power, and everything beside.

But what was strangest in this virgin crew,
  Although her beauty was enough to vex,
After the first investigating view,
  They all found out as few, or fewer, specks
In the fair form of their companion new,
  Than is the custom of the gentle sex,
When they survey, with Christian eyes or Heathen,
In a new face 'the ugliest creature breathing.'

XXXVIII

And yet they had their little jealousies,
  Like all the rest; but upon this occasion,
Whether there are such things as sympathies
  Without our knowledge or our approbation,
Although they could not see through his disguise,
  All felt a soft kind of concatenation,
Like magnetism, or devilism, or what
You please—we will not quarrel about that:

But certain 'tis they all felt for their new
  Companion something newer still, as 'twere
A sentimental friendship through and through,
  Extremely pure, which made them all concur

In wishing her their sister, save a few
   Who wished they had a brother just like her,
Whom, if they were at home in sweet Circassia,
They would prefer to Padisha or Pacha.

XL

Of those who had most genius for this sort
   Of sentimental friendship, there were three,
Lolah, Katinka, and Dudù; in short,
   (To save description) fair as fair can be
Were they, according to the best report,
   Though differing in stature and degree,
And clime and time, and country and complexion;
They all alike admired their new connection.

XLI

Lolah was dusk as India, and as warm;
   Katinka was a Georgian, white and red,
With great blue eyes, a lovely hand and arm,
   And feet so small they scarce seemed made to tread,
But rather skim the earth; while Dudù's form
   Looked more adapted to be put to bed,
Being somewhat large, and languishing, and lazy,
Yet of a beauty that would drive you crazy.

XLII

A kind of sleepy Venus seemed Dudù,
   Yet very fit to 'murder sleep' in those
Who gazed upon her cheek's transcendent hue,
   Her Attic forehead, and her Phidian nose:
Few angles were there in her form, 'tis true,
   Thinner she might have been, and yet scarce lose;
Yet, after all, 'twould puzzle to say where
It would not spoil some separate charm to *pare*.

[140]

She was not violently lively, but
   Stole on your spirit like a May-day breaking;
Her eyes were not too sparkling, yet, half shut,
   They put beholders in a tender taking;
She looked (this simile's quite new) just cut
   From marble, like Pygmalion's statue waking,
The mortal and the marble still at strife,
And timidly expanding into life.

XLIV

Lolah demanded the new damsel's name—
   'Juanna.'—Well, a pretty name enough.
Katinka asked her also whence she came—
   'From Spain.'—'But where *is* Spain?'—'Don't ask
     such stuff,
Nor show your Georgian ignorance—for shame!'
   Said Lolah, with an accent rather rough,
To poor Katinka: 'Spain's an island near
Morocco, betwixt Egypt and Tangier.'

XLV

Dudù said nothing, but sat down beside
   Juanna, playing with her veil or hair;
And looking at her steadfastly, she sighed,
   As if she pitied her for being there,
A pretty stranger, without friend or guide,
   And all abashed, too, at the general stare
Which welcomes hapless strangers in all places,
With kind remarks upon their mien and faces.

XLVI

But here the Mother of the Maids drew near,
   With 'Ladies, it is time to go to rest:
I'm puzzled what to do with you, my dear,'

[141]

She added to Juanna, their new guest:
'Your coming has been unexpected here,
    And every couch is occupied; you had best
Partake of mine; but by tomorrow early
We will have all things settled for you fairly.'

                    XLVII
Here Lolah interposed—'Mamma, you know
    You don't sleep soundly, and I cannot bear
That anybody should disturb you so;
    I'll take Juanna; we're a slenderer pair
Than you would make the half of;—don't say no;
    And I of your young charge will take due care.'
But here Katinka interfered, and said,
'She also had compassion and a bed.'

                    XLVIII
'Besides, I hate to sleep alone,' quoth she.
    The matron frowned:—'Why so?'—'For fear of ghosts,'
Replied Katinka; 'I am sure I see
    A phantom upon each of the four posts;
And then I have the worst dreams that can be,
    Of Guebres, Giaours, and Ginns, and Gouls in hosts.'
The dame replied, 'Between your dreams and you,
I fear Juanna's dreams would be but few.

                    XLIX
'You, Lolah, must continue still to lie
    Alone, for reasons which don't matter; you
The same, Katinka, until by and by;
    And I shall place Juanna with Dudù,
Who's quiet, inoffensive, silent, shy,
    And will not toss and chatter the night through.
What say you, child?'—Dudù said nothing, as
Her talents were of the more silent class;

                    [142]

L

But she rose up, and kissed the matron's brow
  Between the eyes, and Lolah on both cheeks,
Katinka too; and with a gentle bow
  (Curtsies are neither used by Turks nor Greeks)
She took Juanna by the hand to show
  Their place of rest, and left to both their piques,
The others pouting at the matron's preference
Of Dudù, though they held their tongues from deference.

LI

It was a spacious chamber (Oda is
  The Turkish title), and ranged round the wall
Were couches, toilets—and much more than this
  I might describe, as I have seen it all,
But it suffices—little was amiss;
  'Twas on the whole a nobly furnished hall,
With all things ladies want, save one or two,
And even those were nearer than they knew.

LII

Dudù, as has been said, was a sweet creature,
  Not very dashing, but extremely winning,
With the most regulated charms of feature,
  Which painters cannot catch like faces sinning
Against proportion—the wild strokes of nature
  Which they hit off at once in the beginning,
Full of expression, right or wrong, that strike,
And pleasing, or unpleasing, still are like.

LIII

But she was a soft landscape of mild earth,
  Where all was harmony, and calm, and quiet,
Luxuriant, budding; cheerful without mirth,
  Which, if not happiness, is much more nigh it

[143]

Than are your mighty passions and so forth,
  Which some call 'the sublime:' I wish they'd try it:
I've seen your stormy seas and stormy women,
And pity lovers rather more than seamen.

LIV

But she was pensive more than melancholy,
  And serious more than pensive, and serene,
It may be, more than either—not unholy
  Her thoughts, at least till now, appear to have been.
The strangest thing was, beauteous, she was wholly
  Unconscious, albeit turned of quick seventeen,
That she was fair, or dark, or short, or tall;
She never thought about herself at all.

LV

And therefore was she kind and gentle as
  The Age of Gold (when gold was yet unknown,
By which its nomenclature came to pass;
  Thus most appropriately has been shown
'Lucus *a non* lucendo,' *not* what *was*,
  But what *was not*; in a sort of style that's grown
Extremely common in this age, whose metal
The devil may decompose, but never settle:

LVI

I think it may be of 'Corinthian Brass,'
  Which was a mixture of all metals, but
The brazen uppermost). Kind reader! pass
  This long parenthesis: I could not shut
It sooner for the soul of me, and class
  My faults even with your own! which meaneth, Put
A kind construction upon them and me:
But *that* you won't—then don't—I'm not less free.

LVII

'Tis time we should return to plain narration,
  And thus my narrative proceeds:—Dudù,
With every kindness short of ostentation,
  Showed Juan, or Juanna, through and through
This labyrinth of females, and each station
  Described—what's strange—in words extremely few:
I've but one simile, and that's a blunder,
For wordless woman, which is *silent* thunder.

And next she gave her (I say *her*, because
  The gender still was epicene, at least
In outward show, which is a saving clause)
  An outline of the customs of the East,
With all their chaste integrity of laws,
  By which the more a harem is increased,
The stricter doubtless grow the vestal duties
Of any supernumerary beauties.

LIX

And then she gave Juanna a chaste kiss:
  Dudù was fond of kissing—which I'm sure
That nobody can ever take amiss,
  Because 'tis pleasant, so that it be pure,
And between females means no more than this—
  That they have nothing better near, or newer.
'Kiss' rhymes to 'bliss' in fact as well as verse—
I wish it never led to something worse.

In perfect innocence she then unmade
  Her toilet, which cost little, for she was
A child of Nature, carelessly arrayed:
  If fond of a chance to ogle at her glass,

'Twas like the fawn, which, in the lake displayed,
  Beholds her own shy, shadowy image pass,
When first she starts, and then returns to peep,
Admiring this new native of the deep.

And one by one her articles of dress
  Were laid aside; but not before she offered
Her aid to fair Juanna, whose excess
  Of modesty declined the assistance proffered:
Which passed well off—as she could do no less;
  Though by this politesse she rather suffered,
Pricking her fingers with those cursed pins,
Which surely were invented for our sins,—

LXII

Making a woman like a porcupine,
  Not to be rashly touched. But still more dread,
Oh, ye! whose fate it is, as once 'twas mine,
  In early youth, to turn a lady's maid;
I did my very boyish best to shine
  In tricking her out for a masquerade:
The pins were placed sufficiently, but not
Stuck all exactly in the proper spot.

But these are foolish things to all the wise,
  And I love wisdom more than she loves me;
My tendency is to philosophise
  On most things, from a tyrant to a tree;
But still the spouseless virgin Knowledge flies.
  What are we? and whence came we? what shall be
Our ultimate existence? what's our present?
Are questions answerless, and yet incessant.

There was deep silence in the chamber: dim
  And distant from each other burned the lights,
And slumber hovered o'er each lovely limb
  Of the fair occupants: if there be sprites,
They should have walked there in their sprightliest trim,
  By way of change from their sepulchral sites,
And shown themselves as ghosts of better taste
Than haunting some old ruin or wild waste.

LXV

Many and beautiful lay those around,
  Like flowers of different hue, and clime, and root,
In some exotic garden sometimes found,
  With cost, and care, and warmth, induced to shoot.
One with her auburn tresses lightly bound,
  And fair brows gently drooping, as the fruit
Nods from the tree, was slumbering with soft breath,
And lips apart, which showed the pearls beneath.

One with her flushed cheek laid on her white arm,
  And raven ringlets gathered in dark crowd
Above her brow, lay dreaming soft and warm;
  And smiling through her dream, as through a cloud
The moon breaks, half unveiled each further charm,
  As, slightly stirring in her snowy shroud,
Her beauties seized the unconscious hour of night
All bashfully to struggle into light.

LXVII

This is no bull, although it sounds so; for
  'Twas night, but there were lamps, as hath been said.
A third's all pallid aspect offered more
  The traits of sleeping sorrow, and betrayed

[147]

Through the heaved breast the dream of some far shore
   Beloved and deplored; while slowly strayed
(As night-dew, on a cypress glittering, tinges
The black bough), tear-drops through her eyes' dark fringes.

LXVIII

A fourth as marble, statue-like and still,
   Lay in a breathless, hushed, and stony sleep;
White, cold, and pure, as looks a frozen rill,
   Or the snow minaret on an Alpine steep,
Or Lot's wife done in salt,—or what you will;—
   My similes are gathered in a heap,
So pick and choose—perhaps you'll be content
With a carved lady on a monument.

LXIX

And lo! a fifth appears;—and what is she?
   A lady of 'a certain age,' which means
Certainly agèd—what her years might be
   I know not, never counting past their teens;
But there she slept, not quite so fair to see,
   As ere that awful period intervenes
Which lays both men and women on the shelf,
To meditate upon their sins and self.

LXX

But all this time how slept, or dreamed, Dudù?
   With strict inquiry I could ne'er discover,
And scorn to add a syllable untrue;
   But ere the middle watch was hardly over,
Just when the fading lamps waned dim and blue,
   And phantoms hovered, or might seem to hover,
To those who like their company, about
The apartment, on a sudden she screamed out:

LXXI

And that so loudly, that upstarted all
  The Oda, in a general commotion:
Matron and maids, and those whom you may call
  Neither, came crowding like the waves of ocean,
One on the other, throughout the whole hall,
  All trembling, wondering, without the least notion
More than I have myself of what could make
The calm Dudù so turbulently wake.

LXXII

But wide awake she was, and round her bed,
  With floating draperies and with flying hair,
With eager eyes, and light but hurried tread,
  And bosoms, arms, and ankles glancing bare,
And bright as any meteor ever bred
  By the North Pole,—they sought her cause of care,
For she seemed agitated, flushed, and frightened,
Her eye dilated, and her colour heightened.

LXXIII

But what is strange—and a strong proof how great
  A blessing is sound sleep—Juanna lay
As fast as ever husband by his mate
  In holy matrimony snores away.
Not all the clamour broke her happy state
  Of slumber, ere they shook her,—so they say
At least,—and then she, too, unclosed her eyes,
And yawned a good deal with discreet surprise.

LXXIV

And now commenced a strict investigation,
  Which, as all spoke at once, and more than once
Conjecturing, wondering, asking a narration,
  Alike might puzzle either wit or dunce

To answer in a very clear oration.
    Dudù had never passed for wanting sense,
But being 'no orator as Brutus is,'
Could not at first expound what was amiss.

LXXV

At length she said, that in a slumber sound
    She dreamed a dream, of walking in a wood—
A 'wood obscure,' like that where Dante found
    Himself in at the age when all grow good;
Life's half-way house, where dames with virtue crowned
    Run much less risk of lovers turning rude;
And that this wood was full of pleasant fruits,
And trees of goodly growth and spreading roots;

LXXVI

And in the midst a golden apple grew,—
    A most prodigious pippin—but it hung
Rather too high and distant; that she threw
    Her glances on it, and then, longing, flung
Stones and whatever she could pick up, to
    Bring down the fruit, which still perversely clung
To its own bough, and dangled yet in sight,
But always at a most provoking height;—

LXXVII

That on a sudden, when she least had hope,
    It fell down of its own accord before
Her feet; that her first movement was to stoop
    And pick it up, and bite it to the core;
That just as her young lip began to ope
    Upon the golden fruit the vision bore,
A bee flew out, and stung her to the heart,
And so—she woke with a great scream and start.

LXXVIII

All this she told with some confusion and
   Dismay, the usual consequence of dreams
Of the unpleasant kind, with none at hand
   To expound their vain and visionary gleams.
I've known some odd ones which seemed really planned
   Prophetically, or that which one deems
A 'strange coincidence,' to use a phrase
By which such things are settled now-a-days.

LXXIX

The damsels, who had thoughts of some great harm,
   Began, as is the consequence of fear,
To scold a little at the false alarm
   That broke for nothing on their sleeping ear.
The matron, too, was wrath to leave her warm
   Bed for the dream she had been obliged to hear,
And chafed at poor Dudù, who only sighed,
And said, that she was sorry she had cried.

LXXX

'I've heard of stories of a cock and bull;
   But visions of an apple and a bee,
To take us from our natural rest, and pull
   The whole Oda from their beds at half-past three,
Would make us think the moon is at its full.
   You surely are unwell, child! we must see,
To-morrow, what his Highness's physician
Will say to this hysteric of a vision.

LXXXI

'And poor Juanna, too, the child's first night
   Within these walls, to be broke in upon
With such a clamour—I had thought it right
   That the young stranger should not lie alone,

[151]

And, as the quietest of all, she might
    With you, Dudù, a good night's rest have known:
But now I must transfer her to the charge
Of Lolah—though her couch is not so large.'

LXXXII

Lolah's eyes sparkled at the proposition;
    But poor Dudù, with large drops in her own,
Resulting from the scolding or the vision,
    Implored that present pardon might be shown
For this first fault, and that on no condition
    (She added in a soft and piteous tone)
Juanna should be taken from her, and
Her future dreams should be all kept in hand.

She promised never more to have a dream,
    At least to dream so loudly as just now;
She wondered at herself how she could scream—
    'Twas foolish, nervous, as she must allow,
A fond hallucination, and a theme
    For laughter—but she felt her spirits low,
And begged they would excuse her; she'd get over
This weakness in a few hours, and recover.

And here Juanna kindly interposed,
    And said she felt herself extremely well
Where she then was, as her sound sleep disclosed,
    When all around rang like a tocsin bell;
She did not find herself the least disposed
    To quit her gentle partner, and to dwell
Apart from one who had no sin to show,
Save that of dreaming once 'mal à-propos.'

As thus Juanna spoke, Dudù turned round
  And hid her face within Juanna's breast:
Her neck alone was seen, but that was found
  The colour of a budding rose's crest.
I can't tell why she blushed, nor can expound
  The mystery of this rupture of their rest;
All that I know is, that the facts I state
Are true as truth has ever been of late.

Canto VIII, cxxiv–cxxvi

THE 'PIOUS PASTIME'

CXXIV

If here and there some transient trait of pity
  Was shown, and some more noble heart broke through
Its bloody bond, and saved, perhaps, some pretty
  Child, or an agèd, helpless man or two—
What's this in one annihilated city,
  Where thousand loves, and ties, and duties grew?
Cockneys of London! Muscadins of Paris!
Just ponder what a pious pastime war is.

CXXV

Think how the joys of reading a Gazette
  Are purchased by all agonies and crimes:
Or if these do not move you, don't forget
  Such doom may be your own in after-times.
Meantime the taxes, Castlereagh, and debt,
  Are hints as good as sermons, or as rhymes.
Read your own hearts and Ireland's present story,
Then feed her famine fat with Wellesley's glory.

But still there is unto a patriot nation,
  Which loves so well its country and its king,
A subject of sublimest exultation—
  Bear it, ye Muses, on your brightest wing!
Howe'er the mighty locust, Desolation,
  Strip your green fields, and to your harvests cling,
Gaunt famine never shall approach the throne—
Though Ireland starve, great George weighs twenty stone.

Canto XI, xliv–lxvii

THE LITERARY LIFE

XLIV

For downright rudeness, ye may stay at home;
  For true or false politeness (and scarce *that*
Now) you may cross the blue deep and white foam—
  The first the emblem (rarely though) of what
You leave behind, the next of much you come
  To meet. However, 'tis no time to chat
On general topics: poems must confine
Themselves to unity, like this of mine.

XLV

In the great world,—which, being interpreted,
  Meaneth the west or worst end of the city,
And about twice two thousand people bred
  By no means to be very wise or witty,
But to sit up while others lie in bed,
  And look down on the universe with pity,—
Juan, as an inveterate patrician,
Was well received by persons of condition.

[154]

XLVI

He was a bachelor, which is a matter
  Of import both to virgin and to bride,
The former's hymeneal hopes to flatter;
  And (should she not hold fast by love or pride)
'Tis also of some moment to the latter:
  A rib's a thorn in a wed gallant's side,
Requires decorum, and is apt to double
The horrid sin—and what's still worse, the trouble.

But Juan was a bachelor—of arts,
  And parts, and hearts: he danced and sung, and had
An air as sentimental as Mozart's
  Softest of melodies; and could be sad
Or cheerful, without any 'flaws or starts,'
  Just at the proper time: and though a lad,
Had seen the world—which is a curious sight,
And very much unlike what people write.

XLVIII

Fair virgins blushed upon him; wedded dames
  Bloomed also in less transitory hues;
For both commodities dwell by the Thames,
  The painting and the painted; youth, ceruse,
Against his heart preferred their usual claims,
  Such as no gentleman can quite refuse;
Daughters admired his dress, and pious mothers
Inquired his income, and if he had brothers.

The milliners who furnish 'drapery Misses'
  Throughout the season, upon speculation
Of payment ere the honeymoon's last kisses
  Have waned into a crescent's coruscation,

Thought such an opportunity as this is,
  Of a rich foreigner's initiation,
Not to be overlooked—and gave such credit,
That future bridegrooms swore, and sighed, and paid it.

                               L

The Blues, that tender tribe, who sigh o'er sonnets,
  And with the pages of the last Review
Line the interior of their heads or bonnets,
  Advanced in all their azure's highest hue:
They talked bad French or Spanish, and upon its
  Late authors asked him for a hint or two;
And which was softest, Russian or Castilian?
And whether in his travels he saw Ilion?

                               LI

Juan, who was a little superficial,
  And not in literature a great Drawcansir,
Examined by this learned and especial
  Jury of matrons, scarce knew what to answer:
His duties warlike, loving or official,
  His steady application as a dancer,
Had kept him from the brink of Hippocrene,
Which now he found was blue instead of green.

                               LII

However, he replied at hazard, with
  A modest confidence and calm assurance,
Which lent his learned lucubrations pith,
  And passed for arguments of good endurance.
That prodigy, Miss Araminta Smith
  (Who at sixteen translated 'Hercules Furens'
Into as furious English), with her best look,
Set down his sayings in her common-place book.

LIII

Juan knew several languages—as well
  He might—and brought them up with skill, in time
To save his fame with each accomplished belle,
  Who still regretted that he did not rhyme.
There wanted but this requisite to swell
  His qualities (with them) into sublime:
Lady Fitz-Frisky, and Miss Mævia Mannish,
Both longed extremely to be sung in Spanish.

However, he did pretty well, and was
  Admitted as an aspirant to all
The coteries, and, as in Banquo's glass,
  At great assemblies or in parties small,
He saw ten thousand living authors pass,
  That being about their average numeral;
Also the eighty 'greatest living poets,'
As every paltry magazine can show *it's*.

LV

In twice five years the 'greatest living poet,'
  Like to the champion in the fisty ring,
Is called on to support his claim, or show it,
  Although 'tis an imaginary thing.
Even I—albeit I'm sure I did not know it,
  Nor sought of foolscap subjects to be king,—
Was reckoned, a considerable time,
The grand Napoleon of the realms of rhyme.

But Juan was my Moscow, and Faliero
  My Leipsic, and my Mont Saint Jean seems Cain:
'La Belle Alliance' of dunces down at zero,
  Now that the Lion's fallen, may rise again:

[157]

But I will fall at least as fell my hero;
    Nor reign at all, or as a *monarch* reign;
Or to some lonely isle of gaolers go,
With turncoat Southey for my turnkey Lowe.

LVII

Sir Walter reigned before me; Moore and Campbell
    Before and after; but now grown more holy,
The Muses upon Sion's hill must ramble
    With poets almost clergymen, or wholly;
And Pegasus has a psalmodic amble
    Beneath the very Reverend Rowley Powley,
Who shoes the glorious animal with stilts,
A modern Ancient Pistol—by the hilts!

LVIII

Still he excels that artificial hard
    Labourer in the same vineyard, though the vine
Yields him but vinegar for his reward,—
    That neutralised dull Dorus of the Nine;
That swarthy Sporus, neither man nor bard;
    That ox of verse, who *ploughs* for every line:—
Cambyses' roaring Romans beat at least
The howling Hebrews of Cybele's priest.—

LIX

Then there's my gentle Euphues; who, they say,
    Sets up for being a sort of *moral me*;
He'll find it rather difficult some day
    To turn out both, or either, it may be.
Some persons think that Coleridge hath the sway;
    And Wordsworth has supporters, two or three;
And that deep-mouthed Bœotian 'Savage Landor'
Has taken for a swan rogue Southey's gander.

[158]

LX

John Keats, who was killed off by one critique,
  Just as he really promised something great,
If not intelligible, without Greek
  Contrived to talk about the Gods of late,
Much as they might have been supposed to speak.
  Poor fellow! His was an untoward fate;
'Tis strange the mind, that very fiery particle,
Should let itself be snuffed out by an article.

LXI

The list grows long of live and dead pretenders
  To that which none will gain—or none will know
The conqueror at least; who, ere Time renders
  His last award, will have the long grass grow
Above his burnt-out brain, and sapless cinders.
  If I might augur, I should rate but low
Their chances;—they're too numerous, like the thirty
Mock tyrants, when Rome's annals waxed but dirty.

LXII

This is the literary *lower* empire,
  Where the prætorian bands take up the matter;—
A 'dreadful trade,' like his who 'gathers samphire,'
  The insolent soldiery to soothe and flatter,
With the same feelings as you'd coax a vampire.
  Now, were I once at home, and in good satire,
I'd try conclusions with those Janizaries,
And show them *what* an intellectual war is.

LXIII

I think I know a trick or two, would turn
  Their flanks;—but it is hardly worth my while
With such small gear to give myself concern:
  Indeed I've not the necessary bile;

[159]

My natural temper's really aught but stern,
  And even my Muse's worst reproof's a smile;
And then she drops a brief and modern curtsy,
And glides away, assured she never hurts ye.

LXIV

My Juan, whom I left in deadly peril
  Amongst live poets and blue ladies, past
With some small profit through that field so sterile,
  Being tired in time, and neither least nor last,
Left it before he had been treated very ill;
  And henceforth found himself more gaily classed
Amongst the higher spirits of the day,
The sun's true son, no vapour, but a ray.

LXV

His morns he passed in business—which dissected,
  Was like all business, a laborious nothing
That leads to lassitude, the most infected
  And Centaur-Nessus garb of mortal clothing,
And on our sofas makes us lie dejected,
  And talk in tender horrors of our loathing
All kinds of toil, save for our country's good—
Which grows no better, though 'tis time it should.

LXVI

His afternoons he passed in visits, luncheons,
  Lounging, and boxing; and the twilight hour
In riding round those vegetable puncheons
  Called 'Parks,' where there is neither fruit nor flower
Enough to gratify a bee's slight munchings;
  But after all it is the only 'bower,'
(In Moore's phrase) where the fashionable fair
Can form a slight acquaintance with fresh air.

[160]

LXVII

Then dress, then dinner, than awakes the world!
   Then glare the lamps, then whirl the wheels, then roar
Through street and square fast flashing chariots hurled
   Like harnessed meteors; then along the floor
Chalk mimics painting; then festoons are twirled;
   Then roll the brazen thunders of the door,
Which opens to the thousand happy few
An earthly Paradise of 'Or Molu.'

Index of First Lines

[162]